SEED MANAGEMENT

SEED MANAGEMENT

By

Dr. Ashok Kumar

Deptt. of Zoology
Bundelkhand University
Campus Department
Jhansi (India)

DPH

DISCOVERY PUBLISHING HOUSE PVT. LTD.
NEW DELHI-110 002

Published by:
Tilak Wasan
DISCOVERY PUBLISHING HOUSE PVT. LTD.
4383/4B, Ansari Road, Darya Ganj
New Delhi-110 002 (India)
Phone : +91-11-23279245, 43596064-65
Fax : +91-11-23253475
E-mail : parul.wasan@gmail.com
discoverypublishinghouse@gmail.com
web : www.discoverypublishinggroup.com

***First Edition:* 2013**

ISBN: 978-93-5056-302-1

Seed Management

Printed at:
Dynamic Printers
Delhi

Preface

A seed is a small embryonic plant enclosed in a covering called the seed coat, usually with some stored food. It is the product of the ripened ovule of gymnosperm and angiosperm plants which occurs after fertilization and some growth within the mother plant. The formation of the seed completes the process of reproduction in seed plants (started with the development of flowers and pollination), with the embryo developed from the zygote and the seed coat from the integuments of the ovule.

Seeds have been an important development in the reproduction and spread of flowering plants, relative to more primitive plants like mosses, ferns and liverworts, which do not have seeds and use other means to propagate themselves. This can be seen by the success of seed plants (both gymnosperms and angiosperms) in dominating biological niches on land, from forests to grasslands both in hot and cold climates.

The seed of most legume species contains a high proportion of 'hard seeds'. The seed coat of such seeds will not allow the seed to take up moisture and thus to germinate unless it is treated in some way. In the longer term, hard seed will germinate because of the influence of changes in soil temperature and moisture content on the seed coat but with some species this may take several years. For a rapid germination and establishment of seed of less than nine months of age, seed should be treated either by mechanical scarification or by immersion in hot water -both techniques readily suited to commercial practice.

There are often techniques, such as heat treatment or acid scarification but which are more difficult to undertake, especially for large quantities of seed and the lack of appropriate facilities for on farm treatments.

Mechanical scarification can be carried out by abrasing seed with sandpaper in a rotating drum lined with medium grain sandpaper and fitted with a spinning disc that throws seed against the walls of the container. Small quantities of seed can be treated by rubbing the seed between sandpaper. Rubbing seed on a rough cement floor is also effective.

Cultivar purity is the first consideration in seed certification, but other factors such as the absence of weeds and diseases, viability, mechanical purity, and grade are also important. One of the most effective ways to limit the distribution of weeds is to plant weed-free seed. Planting disease-free seed can reduce losses in the same way.

Properly, cleaned and graded seed is easier to plant and gives more uniform stand. Thus, seed certification has been designed not only to maintain genetic purity of superior cultivars, but also to establish and maintain reasonable standards of seed condition and quality.

Seed is a fundamental input for agriculture. Indeed, seed is the single most important input in all crop-based farming systems and a prerequisite for most of the world's food production. More than being the basis of production for the majority of the world's crops, seed determines the upper limit on yield and therefore on the ultimate productivity of all other inputs.

—Author

Contents

CHAPTER – 1

Introduction

Seed is a living product that must be grown, harvested and processed correctly to maximize its viability and subsequent crop productivity. For the yield potential of any rice variety to be realized, good quality seed must be sown. Good quality seed can increase yields by 5-20 per cent. The extent of this increase is directly proportional to the quality of seed that is being sown. Seed quality can be considered as the summation of all factors that contribute to seed performance.

High quality seed enables farmers to attain crops, which have:

- the most economical planting rate;
- a higher percentage of seeds;
- emerging in the field;
- a minimum of replanting;
- a vigorous seedling establishment;
- a more uniform plant stand;
- faster growth rate;

- greater resistance to stress and diseases; and
- uniformity in ripening.

Seed quality is determined by a number of genetic and physiological characteristics. The genetic component involves differences between two or more genetic lines, while differences between seed lots of a single genetic line comprise the physiological component.

The genetic factors that can influence quality include:

- genetic make-up;
- seed size; and
- bulk density

The physical or environmental characteristics include:

- injury during planting and establishment;
- growing conditions during seed development;
- nutrition of the mother plant;
- physical damage during production or storage by either machine or pest;
- moisture and temperature during storage; and
- age or maturity of seed.

Deterioration in seed quality may begin at any point in the plant's development stage from fertilization onward. Seed quality depends upon the physical conditions that the mother plant is exposed during its growth stages, as well as harvesting, processing, storage and planting. Temperature, nutrients and other environmental factors also affect seed development and influence seed quality.

High quality seeds are the result of good production practices, which include:

- proper maintenance of genetic purity;
- good growing conditions;
- proper timing and methods of harvesting;
- appropriate processing during threshing, cleaning and drying;
- appropriate seed storage and seed distribution systems.

The purpose of seed certification is to maintain and make available to farmers, high quality and genetically pure seeds of superior cultivars. Only those cultivars that are of superior genetic makeup, multiplied to maintain purity and identity, are normally eligible for government certification. Certified seed is high in genetic purity, high in germination and vigor, and of good quality (i.e., free from disease and from damaged or immature seeds).

Cultivar purity is the first consideration in seed certification, but other factors such as the absence of weeds and diseases, viability, mechanical purity, and grade are also important. One of the most effective ways to limit the distribution of weeds is to plant weed-free seed. Planting disease-free seed can reduce losses in the same way.

Properly, cleaned and graded seed is easier to plant and gives more uniform stand. Thus, seed certification has been designed not only to maintain genetic purity of superior cultivars, but also to establish and maintain reasonable standards of seed condition and quality.

Seed Testing

Seed samples are collected and submitted for laboratory analysis after drying and processing.

Tests conducted include:

- Varietal purity;
- Weed and other crop seed;
- Inert material;
- Other varieties;
- Red rice;
- Germination; and
- Moisture content.

For seed certification, field inspectors must check:

- Crop land requirements (e.g., previous crop and isolation distances to ensure no; pollen mixes and or volunteers from a different previously planted cultivar);

- The source of the crop's seed (to ensure cultivar purity);
- Sowing dates, pattern, spacing, and rouging (to ensure crop kept clean and free from contamination).
- Purity of cultivar (i.e., no cultivar mixes)
- Harvesting methods (to prevent mixtures)
- Postharvest operations to ensure correct cleaning, drying, sampling, tagging, labeling and sealing.

The techniques of improved pasture establishment from vegetative planting material and from seeding have been described in detail in Technical Bulletin 3. This section covers important aspects of seed management. One of the main reasons for failure or partial success of establishment of improved pastures involves inadequate soil seed contact, use of poor quality seed and insufficient quantities of viable seed sown per hectare. The cost of seed represents usually 10 per cent to 20 per cent of pasture development costs and it is short sighted to compromise the seeding operation.

Seed Treatment

The seed of most legume species contains a high proportion of 'hard seeds'. The seed coat of such seeds will not allow the seed to take up moisture and thus to germinate unless it is treated in some way. In the longer term, hard seed will germinate because of the influence of changes in soil temperature and moisture content on the seed coat but with some species this may take several years. For a rapid germination and establishment of seed of less than nine months of age, seed should be treated either by mechanical scarification or by immersion in hot water-both techniques readily suited to commercial practice.

There are often techniques, such as heat treatment or acid scarification but which are more difficult to undertake, especially for large quantities of seed and the lack of appropriate facilities for on farm treatments.

Mechanical scarification can be carried out by abrasing seed with sandpaper in a rotating drum lined with medium grain sandpaper and fitted with a spinning disc that throws seed against the walls of the container. Small quantities of seed can be treated by rubbing the seed between sandpaper. Rubbing seed on a rough cement floor is also effective.

The alternative is to heat seed in water at 80°C for four minutes and allowing it to dry out. This is the specific recommendation for leucaena seed if less than 12 months old.

Some grasses, particularly signal and Sabi grass require a post harvest period of 9-12 months before providing a high content of viable seed.

Seed Storage

Storage temperature and seed moisture content are the most important factors influencing the deterioration of stored seed.

This is especially important for grass seed where high temperatures and high humidity can quickly reduce seed viability. For instance recorded signal grass germinations have declined from 60 per cent on arrival in Vanuatu in January to 30 per cent in April in cool, non-airconditioned storage. Even under air—conditioning in Vanuatu grass seed should not be stored for more than 3 months, otherwise the quality of pasture establishment will decline.

For short term storage (1-9 months) the temperature and per cent relative humidity should not exceed 30°C and 50 per cent RH or 20°C and 60 per cent RH; for intermediate storage (9-18 months) the ranges are 30°C, 40 per cent RH; or 20°C and 50 per cent RH or 10°C and 60 per cent RH.

On farm seed should be stored in a cool, dry, ventilated room with aluminium reflective insulation under the roof. Seed bags should be off the floor and the area should be rat proof.

When purchasing seed insist on information from a recent seed quality analysis from a recognised laboratory. Always buy the highest germination line possible because this will give you the greatest number of established seedlings for your investment.

In Vanuatu where usually seed establishment conditions are favourable, unlike parts of tropical Australia, a low level of hardseededness in legumes or dormancy in grasses is required. Because potential weed problems exist for any seeded pasture in Vanuatu it is imperative that an adequate number of grass and legume seedlings are established per square metre to compete strongly with weed seedlings. This is the most important single management factor in controlling weeds in an establishing pasture.

New conditions apply for permission to import seed into Vanuatu. This is essential as in excess of 30 tonnes of seed per annum is imported and there are risks of introducing new undesirable weeds or seed of totally unacceptable weeds that already exist here. Also there are risks of introducing live insects.

For longer term storage of small quantities of seed, packages of laminated materials such as layers of polythene, aluminium foil, cellophane or polyester should be used. Polythene alone transmits water vapour and is not recommended for seed storage under high temperature and humidity conditions.

Rhizobial Requirements of Legumes

Most legumes require inoculation with rhizobia that will enable the plants to fix nitrogen from the air. In many cases a specific strain of rhizobium is required e.g. for centro seed, but in others the soil may contain the appropriate rhizobium and inoculation may not be required.

However, even if the soil contains the required rhizobium strain the rate of nodulation and nitrogen fixation will be increased through applying the inoculant in contact with the seed.

The rhizobium is commercially available mixed in a peat culture, which ensures the survival of the rhizobia until seed germination. Improved survival is obtained by using an adhesive or sticker to attach the inoculum to the seed. The most readily available form of sticker is a 10 per cent sugar solution (i.e. 10 gm sugar in 100 ml water). Seed is wetted with the solution and the peat culture mixed with the seed and allowed to dry in the shade - direct sunlight will kill the rhizobium.

The main points to be observed when inoculating seed are:

- make sure that the seed has not been treated with chemical and that containers used do not contain toxic substances such as oil, petrol, chemical pesticides;
- do not mix inoculated seed with acid fertilisers such as superphosphate;
- ensure that the peat culture used is within the expiry period;
- store inoculum in a refrigerator - up to 2 months maximum.
- sow into moist soil.

Spraying a peat/inoculum mix onto established legumes during cloudy weather can partially or completely overcome nodulation failure.

CHAPTER – 2

Seed

A seed is a small embryonic plant enclosed in a covering called the seed coat, usually with some stored food. It is the product of the ripened ovule of gymnosperm and angiosperm plants which occurs after fertilization and some growth within the mother plant. The formation of the seed completes the process of reproduction in seed plants (started with the development of flowers and pollination), with the embryo developed from the zygote and the seed coat from the integuments of the ovule.

Seeds have been an important development in the reproduction and spread of flowering plants, relative to more primitive plants like mosses, ferns and liverworts, which do not have seeds and use other means to propagate themselves. This can be seen by the success of seed plants (both gymnosperms and angiosperms) in dominating biological niches on land, from forests to grasslands both in hot and cold climates.

The term *seed* also has a general meaning that predates the above — anything that can be sown, e.g. "seed" potatoes, "seeds" of corn or sunflower "seeds". In the case of sunflower and corn "seeds", what is sown is the seed enclosed in a shell or hull, and the potato is a tuber.

A typical seed includes three basic parts:

1. an embryo;
2. a supply of nutrients for the embryo; and
3. a seed coat.

The embryo is an immature plant from which a new plant will grow under proper conditions. The embryo has one cotyledon or seed leaf in monocotyledons, two cotyledons in almost all dicotyledons and two or more in gymnosperms. The radicle is the embryonic root. The plumule is the embryonic shoot. The embryonic stem above the point of attachment of the cotyledon(s) is the epicotyl. The embryonic stem below the point of attachment is the hypocotyl.

Within the seed, there usually is a store of nutrients for the seedling that will grow from the embryo. The form of the stored nutrition varies depending on the kind of plant. In angiosperms, the stored food begins as a tissue called the endosperm, which is derived from the parent plant via double fertilization. The usually triploid endosperm is rich in oil or starch and protein. In gymnosperms, such as conifers, the food storage tissue is part of the female gametophyte, a haploid tissue. In some species, the embryo is embedded in the endosperm or female gametophyte, which the seedling will use upon germination. In others, the endosperm is absorbed by the embryo as the latter grows within the developing seed, and the cotyledons of the embryo become filled with this stored food. At maturity, seeds of these species have no endosperm and are termed exalbuminous seeds. Some exalbuminous seeds are bean, pea, oak, walnut, squash, sunflower, and radish. Seeds with an endosperm at maturity are termed albuminous seeds. Most monocots (e.g. grasses and palms) and many dicots (e.g. brazil nut and castor bean) have albuminous seeds. All gymnosperm seeds are albuminous.

The seed coat (or *testa*) develops from the tissue, the integument, originally surrounding the ovule. The seed coat in the mature seed can be a paper-thin layer (e.g. peanut) or something more substantial (e.g. thick and hard in honey locust and coconut). The seed coat helps protect the embryo from mechanical injury and from drying out.

In addition to the three basic seed parts, some seeds have an appendage on the seed coat such an aril (as in yew and nutmeg) or an elaiosome (as in Corydalis) or hairs (as in cotton). There may also be a scar on the seed coat, called the hilum; it is where the seed was attached to the ovary wall by the funiculus.

Seeds are produced in several related groups of plants, and their manner of production distinguishes the angiosperms ("enclosed seeds") from the gymnosperms ("naked seeds"). Angiosperm seeds are produced in a hard or fleshy structure called a fruit that encloses the seeds, hence the name. (Some fruits have layers of both hard and fleshy material). In gymnosperms, no special structure develops to enclose the seeds, which begin their development "naked" on the bracts of cones. However, the seeds do become covered by the cone scales as they develop in some species of conifer.

Seed production in natural plant populations vary widely from year-to-year in response to weather variables, insects and diseases, and internal cycles within the plants themselves. Over a 20-year period, for example, forests composed of loblolly pine and shortleaf pine produced from 0 to nearly 5 million sound pine seeds per hectare. Over this period, there were six bumper seeds, five poor seeds crops, and nine good seed crops, when evaluated in regard to producing adequate seedlings for natural forest reproduction.

Kinds of Seeds

Many structures commonly referred to as "seeds" are actually dry fruits. Sunflower seeds are sold commercially while still enclosed within the hard wall of the fruit, which must be split open to reach the seed. Different groups of plants have other modifications, the so-called *stone* fruits (such as the peach) have a hardened fruit layer (the endocarp) fused to and surrounding the actual seed. Nuts are the one-seeded, hard shelled fruit, of some plants, with an indehiscent seed, such as an acorn or hazelnut.

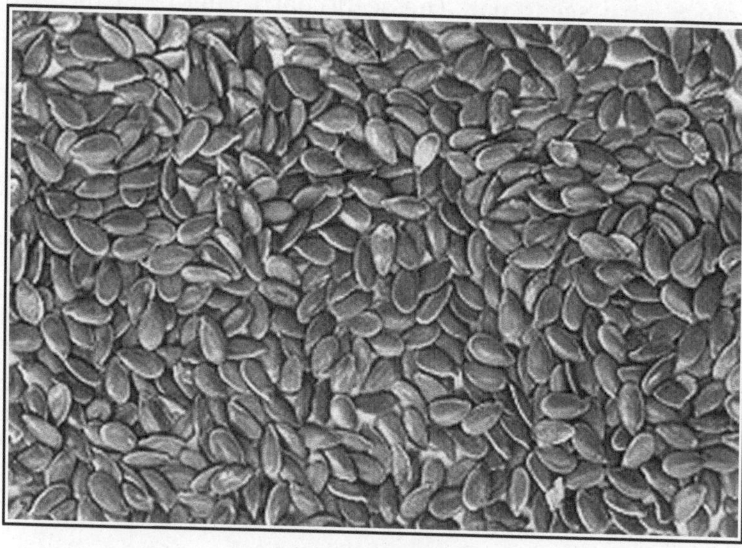

Brown Flax Seeds

Seed Development

The seed, which is an embryo with two points of growth (one of which forms the stems the other the roots) is enclosed in a seed coat with some food reserves. Angiosperm seeds consist of three genetically distinct constituents:

1. the embryo formed from the zygote;
2. the endosperm, which is normally triploid;
3. the seed coat from tissue derived from the maternal tissue of the ovule.

In angiosperms, the process of seed development begins with double fertilization and involves the fusion of the egg and sperm nuclei into a zygote. The second part of this process is the fusion of the polar nuclei with a second sperm cell nucleus, thus forming a primary endosperm. Right after fertilization, the zygote is mostly inactive but the primary endosperm divides rapidly to form the endosperm tissue. This tissue becomes the food that the young plant will consume until the roots have developed after germination or it develops into a hard seed coat. The seed coat forms from the two integuments or outer layers of cells of the ovule, which derive from tissue from the mother plant, the inner integument forms the tegmen and the outer forms the testa. When the seed coat forms from only one layer it is also called the testa, though not all such testa are homologous from one species to the next.

In gymnosperms, the two sperm cells transferred from the pollen do not develop seed by double fertilization but one sperm nucleus unites with the egg nucleus and the other sperm is not used. Sometimes each sperm fertilizes an egg cell and one zygote is then aborted or absorbed during early development. The seed is composed of the embryo (the result of fertilization) and tissue from the mother plant, which also form a cone around the seed in coniferous plants like Pine and Spruce.

The ovules after fertilization develop into the seeds; the main parts of the ovule are the funicle; which attaches the ovule to the placenta, the nucellus; the main region of the ovule were the embryo sac develops, the micropyle; A small pore or opening in the ovule where the pollen tube usually enters during the process of fertilization, and the chalaza; the base of the ovule opposite the micropyle, where integument and nucellus are joined together.

The shape of the ovules as they develop often affects the finale shape of the seeds. Plants generally produce ovules of four shapes: the most common shape is called anatropous, with a curved shape. Orthotropous ovules are straight with all the parts of the ovule lined up in a long row producing an uncurved seed. Campylotropous ovules have a curved embryo sac often giving the seed a tight "c" shape. The last ovule shape is called amphitropous, where the ovule is partly inverted and turned back 90 degrees on its stalk or funicle. In the majority of flowering plants, the zygote's first division is transversely oriented in regards to the long axis, and this establishes the polarity of the embryo. The upper or chalazal pole becomes the main area of growth of the embryo, while the lower or micropylar pole produces the stalk-like suspensor that attaches to the micropyle. The suspensor absorbs and manufacturers nutrients from the endosperm that are utilized during the embryos growth.

The embryo is composed of different parts; the epicotyle will grow into the shoot, the radicle grows into the primary root, the hypocotyl connects the epicotyle and the radicle, the cotyledons form the seed leaves, the testa or seed coat forms the outer covering of the seed. Monocotyledonous plants like corn, have other structures; instead of the hypocotyle-epicotyle, it has a coleoptile that forms the first leaf and connects to the coleorhiza that connects to the primary root and adventitious roots form from the sides. The seeds of corn are constructed with these structures; pericarp, scutellum (single large cotyledon) that absorbs nutrients from the endosperm, endosperm, plumule, radicle, coleoptile and coleorhiza - these last two structures are sheath-like and enclose the plumule and radicle, acting as a protective covering. The testa or seed coats of both monocots and dicots are often marked with patterns and textured markings, or have wings or tufts of hair.

Seed Size and Seed Set

Seeds are very diverse in size. The dust-like orchid seeds are the smallest with about one million seeds per gram; they are often embryonic seeds with immature embryos and no significant energy reserves. Orchids and a few other groups of plants are myco-heterotrophs which depend on mycorrhizal fungi for nutrition during germination and the early growth of the seedling. Some terrestrial Orchid seedlings, in fact, spend the first few years of their life deriving energy from the fungus and do not produce green leaves. At over 20 kg, the largest seed is the coco de mer. Plants that produce smaller seeds can generate many more seeds per flower, while plants with larger seeds invest more resources into those seeds and normally produce fewer seeds. Small seeds are quicker to ripen and can be dispersed sooner, so fall blooming plants often have small seeds. Many annual plants produce great quantities of smaller seeds; this helps to ensure that at least a few will end in a favorable place for growth. Herbaceous perennials and woody plants often have larger seeds, they can produce seeds over many years, and larger seeds have more energy reserves for germination and seedling growth and produce larger, more established seedlings after germination.

Seed Functions

Seeds serve several functions for the plants that produce them. Key among these functions are nourishment of the embryo, dispersal to a new location, and dormancy during unfavorable conditions. Seeds fundamentally are a means of reproduction and most seeds are the product of sexual reproduction which produces a remixing of genetic material and phenotype variability that natural selection acts on.

Embryo Nourishment

Seeds protect and nourish the embryo or young plant. Seeds usually give a seedling a faster start than a sporeling from a spore, because of the larger food reserves in the seed and the multicellularity of the enclosed embryo.

Seed Dispersal

Unlike animals, plants are limited in their ability to seek out favorable conditions for life and growth. As a result, plants have evolved many ways to disperse their offspring by dispersing their seeds (see also vegetative reproduction). A seed must somehow "arrive" at a location and be there at a time favorable for germination and growth. When the fruits open and release their seeds in a regular way, it is called dehiscent, which is often distinctive for related groups of plants, these fruits include; Capsules, follicles, legumes, silicles and siliques. When fruits do not open and release their seeds in a regular fashion they are called indehiscent, which include the fruits achenes, caryopsis, nuts, samaras, and utricles.

Seed dispersal is seen most obviously in fruits; however many seeds aid in their own dispersal. Some kinds of seeds are dispersed while still inside a fruit or cone, which later opens or disintegrates to release the seeds. Other seeds are expelled or released from the fruit prior to dispersal. For example, milkweeds produce a fruit type, known as a *follicle*, that splits open along one side to release the seeds. Iris capsules split into three "valves" to release their seeds.

By Wind (Anemochory)

The seed pod of milkweed (Asclepias syriaca)

- Many seeds (e.g. maple, pine) have a wing that aids in wind dispersal.
- The dustlike seeds of orchids are carried efficiently by the wind.
- Some seeds, (e.g. dandelion, milkweed, poplar) have hairs that aid in wind dispersal.
- Some winged seeds have two, and some have only one wing.

By Water (Hydrochory)

Some plants, such as *Mucuna* and *Dioclea*, produce buoyant seeds termed sea-beans or drift seeds because they float in rivers to the oceans and wash up on beaches.

By Animals (Zoochory)

- Seeds (burrs) with barbs or hooks (e.g. acaena, burdock, dock) which attach to animal fur or feathers, and then drop off later.
- Seeds with a fleshy covering (e.g. apple, cherry, juniper) are eaten by animals (birds, mammals, reptiles, fish) which then disperse these seeds in their droppings.

- Seeds (nuts) which are an attractive long-term storable food resource for animals (e.g. acorns, hazelnut, walnut); the seeds are stored some distance from the parent plant, and some escape being eaten if the animal forgets them.

Myrmecochory is the dispersal of seeds by ants. Foraging ants disperse seeds which have appendages called elaiosomes (e.g. bloodroot, trilliums, Acacias, and many species of Proteaceae). Elaiosomes are soft, fleshy structures that contain nutrients for animals that eat them. The ants carry such seeds back to their nest, where the elaiosomes are eaten. The remainder of the seed, which is hard and inedible to the ants, then germinates either within the nest or at a removal site where the seed has been discarded by the ants. This dispersal relationship is an example of mutualism, since the plants depend upon the ants to disperse seeds, while the ants depend upon the plants seeds for food. As a result, a drop in numbers of one partner can reduce success of the other. In South Africa, the Argentine ant (*Linepithema humile*) has invaded and displaced native species of ants. Unlike the native ant species, Argentine ants do not collect the seeds of *Mimetes cucullatus* or eat the elaiosomes. In areas where these ants have invaded, the numbers of *Mimetes* seedlings have dropped.

Seed Germination

Seed germination is a process by which a seed embryo develops into a seedling. It involves the reactivation of the metabolic pathways that lead to growth and the emergence of the radicle or seed root and plumule or shoot. The emergence of the seedling above the soil surface is the next phase of the plants growth and is called seedling establishment.

Three fundamental conditions must exist before germination can occur:

1. The embryo must be alive, called seed viability.
2. Any dormancy requirements that prevent germination must be overcome.

3. The proper environmental conditions must exist for germination.

Seed viability is the ability of the embryo to germinate and is affected by a number of different conditions. Some plants do not produce seeds that have functional complete embryos or the seed may have no embryo at all, often called empty seeds. Predators and pathogens can damage or kill the seed while it is still in the fruit or after it is dispersed. Environmental conditions like flooding or heat can kill the seed before or during germination. The age of the seed affects its health and germination ability: since the seed has a living embryo, over time cells die and cannot be replaced. Some seeds can live for a long time before germination, while others can only survive for a short period after dispersal before they die.

Seed vigour is a measure of the quality of seed, and involves the viability of the seed, the germination percentage, germination rate and the strength of the seedlings produced.

The germination percentage is simply the proportion of seeds that germinate from all seeds subject to the right conditions for growth. The germination rate is the length of time it takes for the seeds to germinate. Germination percentages and rates are affected by seed viability, dormancy and environmental effects that impact on the seed and seedling. In agriculture and horticulture quality seeds have high viability, measured by germination percentage plus the rate of germination. This is given as a percent of germination over a certain amount of time, 90 per cent germination in 20 days, for example. 'Dormancy' is covered above; many plants produce seeds with varying degrees of dormancy, and different seeds from the same fruit can have different degrees of dormancy. It's possible to have seeds with no dormancy if they are dispersed right away and do not dry (if the seeds dry they go into physiological dormancy). There is great variation amongst plants and a dormant seed is still a viable seed even though the germination rate might be very low.

Environmental conditions effecting seed germination include; water, oxygen, temperature and light.

Three distinct phases of seed germination occur: water imbibition; lag phase; and radicle emergence.

In order for the seed coat to split, the embryo must imbibe (soak up water), which causes it to swell, splitting the seed coat. However, the nature of the seed coat determines how rapidly water can penetrate and subsequently initiate germination. The rate of imbibition is dependent on the permeability of the seed coat, amount of water in the environment and the area of contact the seed has to the source of water. For some seeds, imbibing too much water too quickly can kill the seed. For some seeds, once water is imbibed the germination process cannot be stopped, and drying then becomes fatal. Other seeds can imbibe and lose water a few times without causing ill-effects, but drying can cause secondary dormancy.

Inducing Germination

Scarification which allows water and gases to penetrate into the seed, include methods that physically break the hard seed coats or soften them by chemicals. Means of scarification include soaking in hot water or poking holes in the seed with a pin or rubbing them on sandpaper or cracking with a press or hammer. Soaking the seeds in solvents or acids is also effective for many seeds. Sometimes fruits are harvested while the seeds are still immature and the seed coat is not fully developed and sown right away before the seed coat become impermeable. Under natural conditions seed coats are worn down by rodents chewing on the seed, the seeds rubbing against rocks (seeds are moved by the wind or water currents), by undergoing freezing and thawing of surface water, or passing through an animal's digestive tract. In the latter case, the seed coat protects the seed from digestion, while often weakening the seed coat such that the embryo is ready to sprout when it gets deposited (along with a bit of fertilizer) far from the parent plant. Microorganisms are often effective in breaking down hard seed coats and are sometimes used by people as a treatment, the seeds are stored in a moist warm sandy medium for several months under non-sterile conditions.

Stratification also called moist-chilling is a method to break down physiological dormancy and involves the addition of moisture to the seeds so they imbibe water and then the seeds are subject to a period of moist chilling to after-ripen the embryo. Sowing outside in late summer and fall and allowing to overwinter outside under cool conditions is an effective way to stratify seeds, some seeds respond more favorably to periods of oscillating temperatures which are part of the natural environment.

Leaching or the soaking in water removes chemical inhibitors in some seeds that prevent germination. Rain and melting snow naturally accomplish this task. For seeds planted in gardens, running water is best - if soaked in a container, 12 to 24 hours of soaking is sufficient. Soaking longer, especially in stagnant water that is not changed, can result in oxygen starvation and seed death. Seeds with hard seed coats can be soaked in hot water to break open the impermeable cell layers that prevent water intake.

Other methods used to assist in the germination of seeds that have dormancy include prechilling, predrying, daily alternation of temperature, light exposure, potassium nitrate, the use of plant growth regulators like gibberellins, cytokinins, ethylene, thiourea, sodium hypochlorite plus others. Some seeds germinate best after a fire, for some seeds fire cracks hard seed coats while in other seeds chemical dormancy is broken in reaction to the presence of smoke, liquid smoke is often used by gardeners to assist in the germination of these species.

The origin of seed plants is a problem that still remains unsolved. However, more and more data tends to place this origin in the middle Devonian. The description in 2004 of the proto-seed *Runcaria heinzelinii* in the Givetian of Belgium is an indication of that ancient origin of seed-plants. As with modern ferns, most land plants before this time reproduced by sending spores into the air, that would land and become whole new plants.

The first "true" seeds are described from the upper Devonian, which is probably the theater of their true first evolutionary radiation. The seed plants progressively became one of the major elements of nearly all ecosystems.

Many seeds are edible and the majority of human calories comes from seeds , especially from cereals, legumes and nuts. Seeds also provide most cooking oils, many beverages and spices and some important food additives. In different seeds the seed embryo or the endosperm dominates and provides most of the nutrients. The storage proteins of the embryo and endosperm differ in their amino acid content and physical properties. For example the gluten of wheat, important in providing the elastic property to bread dough is strictly an endosperm protein.

Seeds are used to propagate many crops such as cereals, legumes, forest trees, turfgrasses and pasture grasses. Particularly in developing countries, a major constraint faced is the inadequacy of the marketing channels to get the seed to poor farmers. Thus the use of farmer-retained seed remains quite common.

Poison and Food Safety

While some seeds are edible, others are harmful, poisonous or deadly. Plants and seeds often contain chemical compounds to discourage herbivores and seed predators. In some cases, these compounds simply taste bad (such as in mustard), but other compounds are toxic or break down into toxic compounds within the digestive system. Children, being smaller than adults, are more susceptible to poisoning by plants and seeds.

A deadly poison, ricin, comes from seeds of the castor bean. Reported lethal doses are anywhere from two to eight seeds, though only a few deaths have been reported when castor beans have been ingested by animals.

In addition, seeds containing amygdalin—apple, apricot, bitter almond, peach, plum, cherry, quince, and others—when consumed in sufficient amounts, may cause Cyanide poisoning. Other seeds that contain poisons include annona, cotton, custard apple, datura, uncooked durian, golden chain, horse-chestnut, larkspur, locoweed, lychee, nectarine, rambutan, rosary pea, sour sop, sugar apple, wisteria, and yew. The seeds of the strychnine tree are also poisonous, containing the poison strychnine.

The seeds of many legumes, including the common bean (*Phaseolus vulgaris*), contain proteins called lectins which can cause gastric distress if the beans are eaten without cooking. The common bean and many others, including the soybean, also contain trypsin inhibitors which interfere with the action of the digestive enzyme trypsin. Normal cooking processes degrade lectins and trypsin inhibitors to harmless forms.

List of Edible Seeds

A list of edible seeds here includes seeds that are directly foodstuffs, rather than yielding derived products.

A variety of species can provide edible seeds. Of the six major plant parts, seeds are the most important source of human food. The other five major plant parts are roots, stems, leaves, flowers, and fruits. Most edible seeds are angiosperms, but a few are gymnosperms. The most important seed food source is cereals, followed by legumes, and nuts.

The list is divided into the following categories:

- *Beans* (or *Legumes*) are protein-rich soft seeds.
- *Cereals* (or *grains*) are grass-like crops that are harvested for their dry seeds. These seeds are often ground to make flour. Cereals provide almost half of all calories consumed in the world. Botanically, true cereals are members of the Poaceae or Grass family.
- *Pseudocereals* are cereal crops that are not members of the Poaceae or Grass Family.

- *Nuts* are botanically a specific type of fruit but the term is also applied to many edible seeds that are not botanically nuts.
- *Gymnosperms* produce nut-like seeds but not flowers or fruits.

Beans, also known as legumes or pulses include:

- Lentils have been part of the human diet since the Neolithic period.
- Chickpeas
- Cowpeas
- Dry beans
- Common bean
- Several species of Vigna, such as the lentil
- Fava or broad beans
- Hyacinth bean
- Lablab
- Lentils
- Lupins
- *Moringa oleifera*
- Peas
- Peanuts
- Pigeon peas
- Sterculia
- Velvet beans
- Winged beans
- Yam beans
- Soybeans

Although some beans can be consumed raw, some need to be heated before consumption. In certain cultures, beans that needed heating anyhow were immediatelly prepared as a seed cake. Some beans that needed heating include:

- *Acacia* spp. (e.g. *Acacia aneura* (mulga), *Acacia cowleana*, *Acacia estrophiolata* (ironweed), *Acacia ligulata* (umbrella bush), *Acacia murrayana* (tjuntjula), *Acacia tetragono-phylla* (wakalpulka), *Acacia kempeana* (Witchetty bush), *Acacia coriacea* (Wiry wattle), *Acacia notabilis, Acacia pyrifolia, Acacia tetragonophylla, Acacia victoriae, Acacia sophorae, Acacia stenophylla, Acacia tumida*)

- *Aleurites moluccana*
- *Atriplex nummularia* (Old man saltbush)
- *Panicum* spp. (e.g. *Panicum australiense, Panicum decompositum, Panicum effusum*)
- *Amaranthus mitchellii*
- *Amaranthus grandiflorus*
- *Brachiaria* spp. (e.g. *Brachiaria piligera Brachiaria milliformis*)
- Brachychiton spp. (e.g. *Brachychiton diversifolium Brachychiton gregorii, Brachychiton paradoxum, Brachychiton populneum*)
- *Bruguiera rheedii*
- *Calandrinia balonensis*
- *Canarium australianum*
- *Canavalia maritima*
- *Entada phaseolides*
- *Eragrostris* spp. (Wangunu) (e.g. Eragrostris eriopoda)
- *Eucalyptus leptopoda*
- *Eucalyptus microtheca*
- *Astrelba pectinata* (Mitchell grass)
- *Portulaca oleracea*
- *Portulaca intraterranea*
- *Marsilea drummondii* (Nardoo)
- *Nymphae gigantea*
- *Rhyncharrhena linearis*
- *Themeda australis*

True cereals are the seeds of certain species of grass. Three—maize, wheat and rice—account for about half of the calories consumed by people every year. Grains can be ground to make flour, used as the basis of bread, cake, noodles or other food products. They can also be boiled or steamed, either whole or ground, and eaten as is. Many cereals are present or past staple foods, provided a large fraction of the calories in the places that they are eaten. Cereals include:

- Barley
- Fonio
- Maize (corn)
- Pearl Millet
- Oats
- Palmer's grass
- Rice
- Rye
- Sorghum
- Spelt
- Teff
- Triticale
- Wheat
- Wild rice
- Pseudocereals

Quinoa is not a grass, but its seeds have been eaten for 6000 years.

- Breadnut
- Buckwheat
- Cattail
- Chia
- Flax
- Grain amaranth
- Kañiwa
- Pitseed Goosefoot
- Quinoa
- Wattleseed (also called *acacia seed*)

According to the botanical definition, nuts are a particular kind of seed. Chestnuts, hazelnuts, and acorns are examples of nuts, under this definition. In culinary terms, however, the term is used more broadly to include fruits that are not botanically qualified as nuts, but that have a similar appearance and culinary role. Examples of culinary nuts include almonds, peanuts and cashews.

- Almond
- Beech
- Brazil nut
- Candlenut
- Cashew

Chestnuts, including:

- Chinese Chestnut
- Sweet Chestnut
- Colocynth
- Cucurbita ficifolia
- Filbert
- *Gevuina avellana*

Hickory, including:

- Pecan
- Shagbark Hickory
- *Terminalia catappa*
- Hazelnut
- Indian Beech
- Kola nut
- Macadamia
- Malabar chestnut
- Pistacia
- Mamoncillo
- Maya nut

- Mongongo
- Oak acorns
- Ogbono nut
- Paradise nut
- Pili nut
- Walnut
- Water Caltrop

Nut-like Gymnosperm Seeds

Pine nuts are Gymnosperm seeds that are edible.

- Cycads
- Ginkgo
- *Gnetum gnemon*
- Juniper
- Monkey-puzzle

Pine nuts, including:

- Chilgoza Pine
- Korean Pine
- Stone Pine
- Colorado Pinyon
- Mexican Pinyon
- Single-leaf Pinyon
- Podocarps

Cempedak *Egusi euryale* ferox (Fox nut) *Fluted pumpkin* Hemp seed Jackfruit Lotus seed Malabar gourd Pumpkin seed Sunflower seed.

CHAPTER – 3

Seed and Agriculture

Seed is a fundamental input for agriculture. Indeed, seed is the single most important input in all crop-based farming systems and a prerequisite for most of the world's food production. More than being the basis of production for the majority of the world's crops, seed determines the upper limit on yield and therefore on the ultimate productivity of all other inputs.

Crop genetic diversity is the basis for research and improvement of crop varieties.

Access to a wide range of genetic diversity allows farmers and plant breeders to adapt a crop to heterogeneous and changing environments, developing cultivars with high levels of adaptation to biotic and abiotic stresses and to human preferences. This makes the conservation of genetic resources important in addressing future challenges of research and crop improvement, seeking to intensify agricultural production and increase food supply, and trying to respond to farmers' different requirements and preferences.

In the 1960s the introduction of science based agricultural technologies often combined with governmental subsidies, increased the productivity of agriculture and this became known as the green revolution. What is less known is that for the past fourty years this rapid increase of productivity has largely been sustained in the developing countries. Most of these gains have been in Asia and Latin America. However, there is recent evidence that impacts of varietal improvement in rice, maize-cassava and other crops have now started to show in Sub-Saharan Africa.

In the early green revolution period around 20 per cent of the increase in agricultural production was simply due to an expansion of the area cultivated, and other parts can be attributed to improved agricultural practices and increased use of inputs such as fertilizer and insecticides.

However, for all developing countries some 21 per cent of the growth in yield and about 17 per cent of production growth could be attributed alone to the use of improved seed. Securing the conservation of crop genetic resources and farmers' access to seed of the desired varieties and of good quality is therefore a very important management issue for farmers and a concern for society in order to achieve food security.

Informal Seed

Informal seed systems are central to conserving crop genetic diversity, sustaining farmers' livelihoods and food security, and making small-scale agriculture a productive and viable option. Several authors have pointed out that informal seed systems are mostly based on traditional social alliances and family relations, cast in the context of mutual interdependence and trust, often forming dynamic networks with a high degree of complexity. Still, althoughmany authors have emphasized the role of informal seed exchange for the conservation of crop genetic diversity as well as for the improvement of farmers' seed security, little attention has been given to the detailed study of the mechanisms of informal seed systems, and relatively little is known about the factors and processes that influence and shape small-scale farmers' practices with regards to informal seed exchange. The flow of seeds or farmer-to-farmer exchange of seed is a neglected area of research. There is an urgent need to understand more in detail the process of farmer-to-farmer exchange of seed.

A better understanding of the dynamics of local seed management can contribute to several important areas related to the improvement of supply of quality seed for agricultural production in poor countries, as well as to the conservation of crop genetic diversity in farmers' fields. These include: Better targeting of agricultural research and crop improvement towards the needs and priorities of poor farmers in the developing world:

- Faster and more widespread introduction of improved material by linking the formal and informal sector more effectively;
- Fostering new joint approaches to crop improvement where thecontributions of farmer management is integrated deliberately into the improvement process;
- Assessment of the potentials and problems of *in situ* germplasm conservation.

In most developing countries two different systems of plant genetic resources management have developed. One is an informal plant genetic resource management system based on farmers' local knowledge. The other is a formal, science-based plant genetic resource management system consisting of institutions for plant conservation, breeding and seed multiplication and distribution. In many cases the formal sector evolved as a result of the emphasis in the 1970s and 1980s on formal crop genetic resource management, the science-based approach of the green revolution and the ideas on modernization of agricultural production.

The informal and formal genetic resource management systems are, however, interlinked and the informal sector may for example supply seed derived directly from germplasm from the formal sector (i.e. improved material).

A distinction can be made between seed supplied directly from the formal or the informal sector, and furthermore a distinction can be made between improved material, and land races or creolized material. The latter is a mixture of one or more landraces with improved material or simply improved material that has been cultivated on farm for a number of cropping cycles. In practice it is difficult to distinguish land races from creolized material, and theterm land race will be used to cover farmer produced material without trying to determine if it contains elements of improved material. Seed provided from the formal sector is generally improved seed, but seed from the informal sector can be anywhere on the sliding scale from improved material to creolized and to land races. The use of the term 'improved' when referring to seed from the formal sector is a question of using conventional terminology and does not imply that land races have not been improved by farmers' management.

In developed countries the formal sector is the dominant system for seed supply, crop development and conservation of crop genetic resources. Most crop production in these countries depends on seed of modern varieties provided by the formal seed sector. In many cases the informal seed sector has almost disappeared or serves only hobby-farmers, though in some cases, according to some authors the informal seed sector continues to play a significant role. For example it is reported that only 50 per cent of the total seed demand of overall agricultural crops in Germany is supplied by the formal seed sector, and that in Spain it is as low as 10 per cent, while the same data for Denmark, and the Netherlands and are reported to be 95 and 75 per cent respectively. It should, however, be kept in mind that the apparently low use of the formal sector as seed supplier does not mean that the material is not improved material.

It estimates that around three quarters of the world's farmers use farm-saved seed, and unlike farmers in developed countries or commercial farmers in developing countries, small-scale farmers in the developing world, who produce primarily for their own consumption, often depend almost entirely on themselves or other farmers for seed. In many developing countries, therefore, informal seed sources supply the vast majority of the seed. Within this broad field a number of authors have set out to describe local seed systems and their importance in relation to agricultural production. These and other studies have stressed the importance of informal seed supply in terms of seed security for small-scale farmers in developing countries, for example in years of deficit harvest or in emergency situations.

Although the adoption of improved varieties for a number of food crops in developing countries is significant, the share of the formal sector in the total seed supply remains low. Furthermore, a considerable part of the spread of improved materials has taken place through the informal seed sector, for example as farmer-to-farmer distribution of seed of improved and creolized varieties.

The mechanisms of local seed exchange have important implications in several respects. It is essential for individual farmers to be able to obtain seed of a certain variety and quality in order to secure agricultural production and food supply. However it also has implications of utmost importance in relation to the evolution and conservation of crop genetic diversity.

The literature on seed systems research is diverse and reflects very different approaches to the subject matter. Rather than presenting a disciplinary overview of the literature, it is described from a thematic angle, following three main approaches, namely, the development approach, the biodiversity conservationist approach, and the emergency seed relief approach. The presentation does not focus narrowly on seed, but sees it in the larger context of agricultural development and agricultural research.

Modernisation of Agriculture and the Green Revolution

The re-discovery in the beginning of the 20th century of Gregor Mendel's findings regarding the genetics of plant reproduction triggered the development of modern plant breeding. The advances in plant breeding and other technologies, and their impacts in terms of crop yields, paved the way for formal crop improvement and seed production. Large investments were made in agricultural research.

Increasingly specialized organizations developed in the form of a formal seed sector, composed of specialized public and private enterprises involved in plant breeding, seed production and distribution, and served by a system of legislative standards for seed quality and variety protection. This also brought substantial changes in the role of farmers in crop improvement and conservation of crop genetic resources.

In parallel to plant breeding, the mechanization of agriculture was also fast increasing, and chemical fertilizers and eventually chemical pesticides were developed. The success of science and technology in agricultural modernization in The United States and Europe after the Second World War became a model for development in the third world. Several years of severe food crisis and famine in various parts of the world, in particular in South Asia, led to the initiation of the development of modern crop varieties for developing countries in the 1950s. The success of the efforts, also known as *'the green evolution'*, to increase yields were indisputable and over the ollowing decades world grain production more than doubled due to the spread of new agricultural technologies, in particular modern high-yielding crop varieties and new agricultural practices In view of the initial successes of the green revolution, agricultural development agencies and governments in developing countries sought to stimulate the flow of seed of modern varieties to farmers. In many developing countries, formal sectors for plant breeding, seed production and distribution programmes were established, often with support from international donor agencies, and with public agencies carrying out most of the activities. For the most part, these systems for plant genetic resource management were modelled on the formal seed sectors in industrialized countries, and activities were professionalized and segregated.

In development circles, technology came to be seen as the generator of development and growth. Technology became the point of departure, and the transfer of technology became the dominant approach towards development. The 'ideology of the neutrality of technology' gained currency. According to the latter, any adverse impacts on poor farmers should not be blamed on the inherent nature of the technology but rather on the agrarian structure, the economic policy environment or the agro-ecological conditions under which the technologies are implemented. As scientist comment, instead of striving for crops and cropping systems to be finely in tune with their environment through natural balance, environments were increasingly adapted to the requirements of the crops.

Research station technologies were viewed as superior to farmer practices since crops performed better on-station with standardized inputs. The failure of modern varieties to spread into marginal areas was thought to be rooted in the conservatism and backwardness of traditional farmers. New and superior technologies were envisioned to be adopted first by a few, more progressive farmers, in order to subsequently filter down to the smaller, more traditional farmers, as they realized the benefits gained by the early adopters.

Technological and economical determinist approaches to technology diffusion assume that a technology will spread almost by itself if it is technologically superior to, or more profitable than, existing technologies. However, experience has shown that though these factors are important, they are by no means a guarantee for success. Most technologies that fulfil these criteria have no or very little practical impact, and often it can be observedthat the technology that achieves widespread adoption is not the best from a technological stand point, nor necessarily the most profitable. Modern approaches to technology diffusion stress the importance of conceptualising technology diffusion as a social process, where people's perceptions and networks play a crucial role. In addition, when the technologies are aimed at resource poor people, experience also highlights the importance of involving the people early in the process in order to adapt the development to their particular situation.

The Challenge of Reaching Farmers in Marginal Areas

Some have argued that international agricultural research is organized in a way which creates structures that are frequently indifferent and insensitive to the needs of small farmers. Another way of putting this could be that the focus of international agricultural research organizations on the production of global public goods, such as generally applicable technologies, has not been able to sufficiently address more local needs or preferences.

The Green Revolution technologies were particularly successful in favourable environments which were adequate for the improved germplasm that was available at that time. In particular this was the case in the irrigated areas in Asia and in Latin America. The improved germplasm available at the beginning of the green revolution was not well adapted to the production conditions, for example, in large parts of Africa.

This limitation was further aggravated by the fact that when artificial fertilizer is applied, cereal landraces often grow too tall and lodge. In many cases this meant that unless improved germplasm was used, farmers could not use chemical fertilizer to increase productivity in their landraces. In less favourable and marginal areas, where production conditions are usually more complex and more risk prone, the green revolution and the formal seed sector have generally had considerably less success. Low soil fertility, frequently occurring droughts, inundations or other climatic hazards reduce the productivity of the crop.

Likewise, access to agricultural inputs like capital, land, labour, water, and fertilizer, is generally limited, more expensive, and more variable due to bad roads and remote markets. In these conditions farmers may lack cash to buy seed. In addition, higher seed quality may not be expressed in higher yields because of other limiting factors, and the purchase of expensive seed may not be considered economical.

Farmers in these areas may grow a wider range of locally adapted varieties with different characteristics. Varieties that are suitable for favourable high-input conditions may not prove the best option for low-input conditions in these marginal areas. Moreover, modern varieties that are bred for high yield may not serve the many different purposes for which a subsistence farmer produces a crop, such as special preferences for home consumption as well as the need for secondary products. Farmers in marginal areas often have different needs and require varieties with multiple characteristicsin particular combinations. This can be difficult to address through formal seed programmes.

Many developing country governments and international development agencies have until recently only supported formal sector institutions forplant genetic resources, and have linked credit, subsidies, research and extension to the adoption of modern varieties. The introduction of Structural Adjustment Programmes in the 1990s reduced, or in many cases completely reintroduction moved, the subsidies for this kind of agriculture and has probably increasedthe number of farmers unable to take advantage of modern crop improvement.

Furthermore, in several countries public sector programmes have faced a series of problems, including severe lack of resources, and as a result they have often produced less than expected. At the same time private sector seed enterprises have encountered high transaction costs and inappropriate legislatory frameworks. In many regards, NGOs have therefore been seen as an important complement and go-between for the strengthening of linkages between the formal seed sector and farmers.

However, not all NGOs have been equally successful in this role. Though also acknowledging several strengths of NGOs, the authors note that operations are generally small-scale and depend heavily on external funding. Furthermore, in severalcases they lack technical expertise, and rather than being innovative, activities appear often to be moulded after those of the formal seed sector.

The diminishing support from governments for farmers is further aggravated by the increased use of intellectual property rights related to crop improvement. Previously a lot of agricultural research was done in public research institutions and there was a relatively free flow of new technologies, but with the advent of biotechnology, new discoveries are more frequently protected by intellectual property rights and the improvements in productivity are likely to take even longer to reach small scale farmers in developing countries.

The importance of seed regulations and legislatory frameworks in relation to efforts to support and strengthen farmers' access to seed of diverse varieties is increasingly being acknowledged, and attention to these aspects has grown significantly. Meanwhile, other approaches have emerged which focus more on the facilitation of farmers' access to seed within local contexts, for example, 'seed vouchers and fairs'.

Advances in agricultural productivity have not only benefited farmers. The prices of agricultural products have fallen over the last decades, and consumers are the largest beneficiaries of the production increase. Some smallscale farmers, particularly in less favourable agro-ecological regions, whowere not able to increase their productivity sufficiently to compensate for falling prices may in fact be worse off today. In summary, therefore, the science-driven increase in agricultural productivity has hugely benefitd consumers, and also benefited the farmers who have the capacity to increase their productivity. However, effectively reaching farmers in more marginal and more remote areas remains a challenge.

Since the beginning of agriculture farmers have domesticated and developed crops, adapting them to diverse environments and specific human preferences through thousands of years of selection and experimentation . Farmers' crop improvement experimentation, as well as the management, production and exchange of crop genetic resources by and amongst farmers are often referred to as informal seed systems, local seed systems or farmers' seed systems. In these, crop improvement, seed supply and conservation perspectives are combined at the local level in farmers' strategies for local crop development. The adaptation and improvement of varieties, seed production, utilization and exchange, as well as the conservation of crop genetic resources, are all integrated activities in these systems.

They are part of the local agricultural system and are usually carried out on the same farm through processes that are based on local knowledge accumulated and used in the community through generations.

The point of departure for this approach is the focus on seed as an important source of germplasm and its role in small-scale agriculture as well as in the evolution of crop genetic diversity and in crop improvement initiatives.

During the last decades concerns about the loss of biodiversity have increased substantially and *genetic erosion* has become a much debated issue, particularly since a diverse set of genetically variable crop landraces has been replaced by a few, genetically uniform, high-yielding varieties.

The increasing pressure on land and labour increases the importance of yield as a selection criterion for farmers, leading to intensified crop production, the adoption of improved varieties with higher yield potentials, the use of more inputs, and the planting of fewer varieties on the farm. Fading cultural diversity and traditions have also been associated with the increasing disappearanceof local cultivars.

Concerns about the loss of plant genetic resources are especially valid in areas of crop domestication, where diversity is concentrated and where farmers maintain not only seed of local varieties of ancestral crop populations but also the human knowledge and behavioural practices that have shaped this diversity for generations.

In many regions local cultivars tend to be left to the more marginal, riskprone habitats and ethnological niches for which the improved varieties are less suitable. Though traditional varieties tend to be sturdier, the tendency to focus their use on marginal lands increases the risk of losing some of these varieties in a bad year.

Some argue that low input farming systems may be particularly subject to genetic vulnerability because of pests and tropical conditions, weak infrastructure and economic marginality. Anthropologists and others have argued that crop genetic diversity is one of the principal means that farmers in low input farming systems use in order to protect production, for example planting several varieties of the same crop as a way of confronting risks and heterogeneous production conditions. From this perspective the loss of crop genetic diversity may therefore leave local cultivators even more vulnerable.

From a social interactionist perspective, local technical knowledge, skills and capacities to manage plant genetic resources are embedded in the cultural, ecological and sociological context of the community. Farmers' local experimentations are not based on scientific theoretical models, but emerge from strong interests in and knowledge of practical local application that provide options for improving their livelihoods.

Modern theories on knowledge argue that science and technology are socially constructed and embody social relations. The development and uptake of scientific and technological knowledge rely upon and modify existing modes of communication and organisational relations. It is by no means a passive process. Rather, it must be considered an active process, an interaction between various agents within particular cultural and organisational contexts, during which the technology may be adapted and transformed, influenced by a series of social and cultural factors.

Local institutions for managing plant genetic resources only seldom take the shape of organizations. They commonly consist of shared norms and practices within a community or ethnic group of people. While the natural resource management by local institutions is often associated with conflict over access and use, plant genetic resources are renewable and are therefore seldom the cause of conflict over access at the local level. Plant genetic resource management is largely the product of social processes and institutions in the community. When these change it is likely also to have an effect on local plant genetic resource management.

In general, studies investigating these aspects at the local level have often portrayed small-scale farmers as the caretakers of important crop genetic resources who continue to maintain and cultivate diverse varieties. However, most small-scale farmers do not maintain crop genetic resources merely for the sake of conservation. Rather, it appears that many farmers give social value to local resources and make special use of diverse crop varieties, either for consumption purposes or as a means of confronting heterogeneous agricultural conditions.

Similarly, the ability of local seed management practices to adapt varieties to specific cultural, economic and social requirements through the application of farmers' knowledge and skills has been documented; Museo Nacional de Cultural Populares, 2002; Orlove and Brush, 1996). In many cases decisions regarding varietal choice depend on multiple considerations, not just on yield. As Orlove and Brush (1996) point out, such issues can be illuminated by in-depth, qualitative studies.

Seed Relief Approach

The seed relief approach grew out of efforts to address seed security in connection to disaster or emergency contexts.

Obviously inspiration was found in food relief programmes in such situations, with the idea that seed relief would contribute to the restoration of local food production.

Originally seed relief interventions were based on the assumption that no seed were available in the affected region. The response was therefore to bring in large quantities of seed of the most important crops and simply distribute it. Later it was found that in fact, the assumption that the problem was one of seed availability was not always correct. Studies showed that often local seed systems were quite resilient, even under very extreme circumstances.

In some emergency situations (e.g. the civil war in Rwanda) bean seed was in fact available in the local seed system, and some farmers managed to plant and harvest in spite of the war and its devastating effects on society. These revelations showed that farmers' problems acquiring seed during crisis were not necessarily due to lack of seed availability. Instead, it seems that farmers' problems in many cases stem from difficulties of access, because the crisis has destroyed social networks (as in the case of Rwanda), thereby disrupting the customary channels for informal seed acquisitions, or because farmers simply lack the means with which to acquire the seed, for example through purchase or barter.

A new 'paradigm' for seed aid interventions has therefore emerged, shifting the focus from merely concentrating on direct seed aid distribution, to a broader approach more oriented towards agricultural rehabilitation and development Acute stress normally refers to a sudden and very violent form of crisis which affects large numbers of people in large areas, such as natural disasters or war. Chronic stress, on the other hand, refers to a constant situation of vulnerability and crisis, for example, very difficult agro-ecological and/or socioeconomic conitions. Chronic stress is closely linked to severe poverty and may not affect all groups equally.

Seed relief in the form of direct distribution of seed brought in from elsewhere has been criticized in a number of other respects. Repeated relief interventions in the same area have turned out often to be due to a misinterpretation of the situation, that is, where a case of chronic stress has been interpreted as an acute stress. In some cases, such repeated emergency seed interventions have led to seed aid dependency and the destruction of local seed systems.

Seed relief interventions have also been criticized for not always presenting appropriate crops or varieties and for not leaving farmers sufficient choice. In some cases it has even been criticized as an unfair or 'back-door' method for promoting modern varieties. Similarly the introduction of large quantities of seed from elsewhere, for example of modern crop varieties, has been associated with risks for local crop genetic diversity, and finally, seed relief interventions have been seen as inappropriately benefiting certain actors from the formal sector, for instance by providing opportunities for corruption.

The direct seed distribution approach is also sometimes called the *Seeds and Tools approach*. It has been criticized in a number of regards: for not always being based on, for example, a proper assessment of the problem (e.g. availability vs. accessibility), which in turn can result in aid dependency for being based on a negative perception of farmer seed systems and for benefiting other sectors more than the intended farmers, such as the formal, commercial sector or the use of inappropriate distribution channels.

As an alternative to the Seeds and Tools approach, agricultural rehabilitation and development tends towards interventions that strengthen existing seed systems and with that the linkages between the formal and informal seed sectors. New strategies emphasize working to understand and strengthen local seed systems, and on integrating relief and development approaches in seed interventions. Rather than focusing solely on direct seed distribution, interventions now try to place grater emphasis on strengthening seed systems from the inside.

Local Knowledge

The various ideas and practices that form part of farmers' seed management can be considered a form of local knowledge – a central concern of many anthropological studies. However, knowledge is also an important field of theory and study in itself, where elements from many disciplines including philosophy, psychology, and anthropology can play a role. Approaches within theory on knowledge can tentatively be divided into two; those that focus mainly on social aspects as distinct from those that relate to cognitive aspects.

The former have focused on issues related to power, how power influences what is considered knowledge, and how discourses on knowledge reproduce power relations. Another important contribution has been the recognition that knowledge is not unitary and systematized, either for the individual, or for the social group; on the contrary, knowledge is fragmentary, diffuse, and multi-layered. Considerations of power and interface are central to many studies involving local people's negotiations with government officials or representatives of private companies. Certain schools of anthropology have, in particular, stressed the usefulness of cognitive theories of knowledge. This has been convincingly argued by the scientists, who underline the limitations of relyingon overly linguistic models of knowledge.

This and other analytical aspects of local knowledge, in particular the communication and negotiation of local understandings, and some of the analytical and methodological implications these imply, are discussed further in Chapter six. This is followed by a presentation and discussion of several aspects of local seed concepts and practices in the study area.

Collective Action

As an analytical concept, collective action has been particularly useful in the study of social movements and the management by multiple actors of public goods or common resources such as forests, fisheries, rangelands, irrigation. However, though crop genetic resources are broadly regarded as a public good, they are very different from other natural resource public goods for which the main problem is over-use. The case of crop genetic resources is quite the opposite - in fact, for many landraces and wild relatives, their conservation is often entirely dependent on their continued use and from a conservation point of view, one might say, theore they are used the better.

Most definitions of collective action share the notion that it necessarily involves multiple actors and is directed towards the achievement of certain *Conceptual framework and methodological strategy* common interests or goals. While the definition of what constitutes the collective, and to what degree the actions it takes can be said to represent a common purpose, remain highly debated, a large body of research has documented the processes by which collective organisation emerges and constitutes itself. This literature gives attention to the rise and functioning of both formal and informal organisations. Moreover, close attention has been paid tohow collectivities have developed that concern themselves with sets of rights and responsibilities related to the use of common resources.

On a more theoretical level, the study of collective action is marked by a divide between those who are interested in social movements as distinct sociocultural entities with a common identity, and those who take their point of departure as the lived experiences and agency of multiple social actors who negotiate to form coalitions that are continuously being reshaped. *Social embeddedness* Farmer seed transactions can be regarded as an economic practice, involving the exchange of a good between two parties. Rational choice theory has played an important role in the development of economic theory and in several respects has contributed greatly to the understanding of economic phenomena.

However, with regard to the study of the practices of economic actors at a more specific level, various critics have pointed to the limitations of theories based on utility maximization. In particular the critique has been directed at the view of actors as independent, 'atomized' and 'rational' decisionmakers with little or no concern for the role of human emotions, social interaction and networks.

Seed transactions can be looked at from a market perspective. In much economic theory a competitive market is viewed as being constituted by a large number of consumers and suppliers who do not influence market dynamics individually. Furthermore, it is often assumed that the actors have perfect information, and that social relations do not significantly influence actors in their transactions. Yet, many detailed studies of social behaviour in real market situations seriously question these assumptions. For example, distances himself from the utilitarian theories of classical and neo-classical economics, and discards the idea of economic behaviour as something heavily embedded in pre-market societies which unfolds and becomes moreautonomous as modernization occurs. As an alternative, he proposes a more integrated view of human actors capable of processing information and experience and acting upon it, but who do not exist independently of the social context of which they form a part.

From an analytical point of view, farmers' seed exchanges can be regarded as interactions in which social capital is mobilized. The concept of social capital has been much debated and used in many different ways to deal with the social aspects of economic practice. Putnam defines social capital as different forms or institutions of social organization that allow individuals to coordinate and pursue interests for their mutual benefit. Putnam furthermore posits a clear relation between the amount of social capital and the level of economic development and democracy in any given society.

While Putnam's work has played an important role in popularising the concept of social capital and has been widely used, among others by the World Bank, it has also been criticized by many for being misleading and for obscuring the role of power.

Social capital has also been described as the result of institutional and individual or collective investments in the reproduction of social relationships that are directly usable in the short or long term. According to Bourdieu, social capital is constantly reproduced through a process in which goods, favours, information, etc. are continuously exchanged as a means of recognizing and affirming social relations and group membership.

Others, such as the economists Marcel Fafchamps and Bart Minten, distinguish between different meanings of social capital according to their origin and types of trust. According to researchers, social capital can be seen, on one hand, as "a 'stock' of trust and an emotional attachment to a group or society at large that facilitate the provision of public goods"; they call this generalized trust. On the other hand, social capital can also take the form of "an individual asset that benefits a single individual or firm", which they refer to as personalized trust.

Other uses of the term merely signal awareness of the significance of social aspects in relation to economic or political processes, without actually contributing to an improved understanding of the issues in question. A related view is that social capital is no more than resources that are obtained through social relations and networks. Another interpretation is that social capital must be understood as the *ability* of actors to use social networks in order to mobilize resources, and not as the actual resources themselves. Furthermore social capital is often viewed as an asset and in some regards also a constraint. farmers mobilize social networks in order to negotiate favourable terms for seed transactions and to acquire maize seed with favoured characteristics.

Trust

As a good, seed lacks transparency. That is, the person acquiring the seed cannot know the characteristics of the plant the seed may produce merely by looking at it, and therefore must rely on the information provided by the seed supplier. This makes trust an important issue in seed transactions.

Trust is relationally and culturally constructed. The notion of trust is often used to describe the expectation or confidence one has that someone will act in a particular way, for example with honesty or sincerity. Different categories of trust have been discussed, and it has also been pointed out that, while trust is generally regarded as something positive and desirable, it can, under certain circumstances, also be regarded as something negative, depending on one's interpretation of the context.

With regard to transaction and social exchange it has been noted that the cultivation and use of trust and trust relations tends to grow in importance under different conditions of risk and uncertainty. Thus, the notion of trust appears to be able to contribute to a feeling of security, when social actors are faced with circumstances they perceive to be risk-prone. This is because the use of relations of trust in connection to commercial exchange, envelopes the exchange in a web of obligations and holds the seller's network hostage to appropriate role performance in relation to the transaction.

Trust and reciprocity appear to be quite closely linked. While trust can lead to relations of reciprocity, reciprocity can also lead to trust.

Transaction Costs

The concept of transaction costs is used to refer to costs incurred in the course of carrying out an economic exchange. Transaction cost theory is part of what has come to be known as new institutional economics. This line of economic theory expands neo-classical economic theories by incorporating property rights and transaction costs into neo-classical economics to explain economic behaviour.

Within the framework of standard transaction cost theory, transaction costs are often divided into different categories. Search or information costs refer to costs that are incurred while exploring whether the required good is to be found on the market, its costs, providers, and so forth. Bargaining or negotiation costs are the costs of negotiating and arriving at an agreement with the other party, as well as carrying out the transaction. Finally, the term enforce ment costs is used to refer to the costs of ensuring that the other party keeps his/her part of the agreement, and, if necessary, of taking action to this effect.

While new institutional economics places a stronger emphasis on empirical testing than, for example, standard neo-classical economics, it also has strong roots in rational choice theory. Some authors argue that this does not change the fact that transaction costs are difficult to measure in any objective way, and that the issue of what constitutes a transaction cost or not is specific to the circumstances and the parties involved.

In this chapter, the concept of transaction costs is used, in a broad sense, as an entry point for examining what, from a farmer's perspective, is regarded as a cost or a sacrifice incurred in relation to maize seed exchanges. It is argued that in farmer-to-farmer seed transactions the transaction costs are perceived by the farmers to be negligible.

CHAPTER – 4

Germination

Germination is the process in which a plant or fungus emerges from a seed or spore and begins growth. The most common example of germination is the sprouting of a seedling from a seed of an angiosperm or gymnosperm. However the growth of a sporeling from a spore, for example the growth of hyphae from fungal spores, is also germination. In a more general sense, germination can imply anything expanding into greater being from a small existence or germ.

Germination is the growth of an embryonic plant contained within a seed; it results in the formation of the seedling. The seed of a higher plant is a small package produced in a fruit or cone after the union of male and female sex cells. All fully developed seeds contain an embryo and, in most plant species some store of food reserves, wrapped in a seed coat. Some plants produce varying numbers of seeds that lack embryos, these are called empty seeds, and never germinate. Most seeds go through a period of quiescence where there is no active growth; during this time the seed can be safely transported to a new location and/or survive adverse climate conditions until circumstances are favourable for growth. Quiescent seeds are ripe seeds that do not germinate because they are subject to external environmental conditions that prevent the initiation of metabolic processes and cell growth. Under favourable conditions, the seed begins to germinate and the embryonic tissues resume growth, developing towards a seedling.

Factors Affecting Seed Germination

Seed germination depends on both internal and external conditions. The most important external factors include temperature, water, oxygen and sometimes light or darkness. Various plants require different variables for successful seed germination, often this depends on the individual seed variety and is closely linked to the ecological conditions of a plant's natural habitat. For some seeds, their future germination response is affected by environmental conditions during seed formation; most often these responses are types of seed dormancy.

Water - is required for germination. Mature seeds are often extremely dry and need to take in significant amounts of water, relative to the dry weight of the seed, before cellular metabolism and growth can resume. Most seeds need enough water to moisten the seeds but not enough to soak them. The uptake of water by seeds is called imbibition, which leads to the swelling and the breaking of the seed coat. When seeds are formed, most plants store a food reserve with the seed, such as starch, proteins, or oils. This food reserve provides nourishment to the growing embryo. When the seed imbibes water, hydrolytic enzymes are activated which break down these stored food resources into metabolically useful chemicals. After the seedling emerges from the seed coat and starts growing roots and leaves, the seedling's food reserves are typically exhausted; at this point photosynthesis provides the energy needed for continued growth and the seedling now requires a continuous supply of water, nutrients, and light.

Oxygen - is required by the germinating seed for metabolism. Oxygen is used in aerobic respiration, the main source of the seedling's energy until it grows leaves. Oxygen is an atmospheric gas that is found in soil pore spaces; if a seed is buried too deeply within the soil or the soil is waterlogged, the seed can be oxygen starved. Some seeds have impermeable seed coats that prevent oxygen from entering the seed, causing a type of physical dormancy which is broken when the seed coat is worn away enough to allow gas exchange and water uptake from the environment.

Temperature - affects cellular metabolic and growth rates. Seeds from different species and even seeds from the same plant germinate over a wide range of temperatures. Seeds often have a temperature range within which they will germinate, and they will not do so above or below this range. Many seeds germinate at temperatures slightly above room-temperature 60-75°F (16-24°C), while others germinate just above freezing and others germinate only in response to alternations in temperature between warm and cool. Some seeds germinate when the soil is cool 28-40°F (-2 -4°C), and some when the soil is warm 76-90°F (24-32°C). Some seeds require exposure to cold temperatures (vernalization) to break dormancy. Seeds in a dormant state will not germinate even if conditions are favourable. Seeds that are dependent on temperature to end dormancy have a type of physiological dormancy. For example, seeds requiring the cold of winter are inhibited from germinating until they take in water in the fall and experience cooler temperatures. Four degrees Celsius is cool enough to end dormancy for most cool dormant seeds, but some groups, especially within the family Ranunculaceae and others, need conditions cooler than -5°C. Some seeds will only germinate after hot temperatures during a forest fire which cracks their seed coats; this is a type of physical dormancy.

Most common annual vegetables have optimal germination temperatures between 75-90°F (24-32°C), though many species (e.g. radishes or spinach) can germinate at significantly lower temperatures, as low as 40°F (4°C), thus allowing them to be grown from seed in cooler climates. Suboptimal temperatures lead to lower success rates and longer germination periods.

A Germinated Seeling (*Eranthis Hyemalis*) Emerges from the Ground

Light or darkness - can be an environmental trigger for germination and is a type of physiological dormancy. Most seeds are not affected by light or darkness, but many seeds, including species found in forest settings, will not germinate until an opening in the canopy allows sufficient light for growth of the seedling.

Scarification mimics natural processes that weaken the seed coat before germination. In nature, some seeds require particular conditions to germinate, such as the heat of a fire (e.g., many Australian native plants), or soaking in a body of water for a long period of time. Others need to be passed through an animal's digestive tract to weaken the seed coat enough to allow the seedling to emerge.

Some live seeds are dormant and need more time, and/ or need to be subjected to specific environmental conditions before they will germinate. Seed dormancy can originate in different parts of the seed, for example, within the embryo; in other cases the seed coat is involved. Dormancy breaking often involves changes in membranes, initiated by dormancy-breaking signals. This generally occurs only within hydrated seeds. Factors affecting seed dormancy include the presence of certain plant hormones, notably abscisic acid, which inhibits germination, and gibberellin, which ends seed dormancy. In brewing, barley seeds are treated with gibberellin to ensure uniform seed germination for the production of barley malt.

Seedling Establishment

In some definitions, the appearance of the radicle marks the end of germination and the beginning of "establishment", a period that ends when the seedling has exhausted the food reserves stored in the seed. Germination and establishment as an independent organism are critical phases in the life of a plant when they are the most vulnerable to injury, disease, and water stress. The germination index can be used as an indicator of phytotoxicity in soils. The mortality between dispersal of seeds and completion of establishment can be so high that many species have adapted to produce huge numbers of seeds.

Germination Rate

In agriculture and gardening, the germination rate describes how many seeds of a particular plant species, variety or seedlot are likely to germinate. It is usually expressed as a percentage, e.g., an 85 per cent germination rate indicates that about 85 out of 100 seeds will probably germinate under proper conditions. The germination rate is useful for calculating the seed requirements for a given area or desired number of plants.

Dicot Germination

The part of the plant that first emerges from the seed is the embryonic root, termed the radicle or primary root. It allows the seedling to become anchored in the ground and start absorbing water. After the root absorbs water, an embryonic shoot emerges from the seed. This shoot comprises three main parts: the cotyledons (seed leaves), the section of shoot below the cotyledons (hypocotyl), and the section of shoot above the cotyledons (epicotyl). The way the shoot emerges differs among plant groups.

Epigeous

In epigeous (or epigeal) germination, the *hypocotyl* elongates and forms a hook, pulling rather than pushing the cotyledons and apical meristem through the soil. Once it reaches the surface, it straightens and pulls the cotyledons and shoot tip of the growing seedlings into the air. Beans, tamarind, and papaya are examples of plants that germinate this way.

Hypogeous

Another way of germination is hypogeous (or hypogeal), where the epicotyl elongates and forms the hook. In this type of germination, the cotyledons stay underground where they eventually decompose. Peas, for example, germinate this way.

Monocot Germination

In monocot seeds, the embryo's radicle and cotyledon are covered by a coleorhiza and coleoptile, respectively. The coleorhiza is the first part to grow out of the seed, followed by the radicle. The coleoptile is then pushed up through the ground until it reaches the surface. There, it stops elongating and the first leaves emerge.

Precocious Germination

While not a class of germination, precocious germination refers to seed germination before the fruit has released seed. The seeds of the green apple commonly germinate in this manner.

Pollen Germination

Another germination event during the life cycle of gymnosperms and flowering plants is the germination of a pollen grain after pollination. Like seeds, pollen grains are severely dehydrated before being released to facilitate their dispersal from one plant to another. They consist of a protective coat containing several cells (up to 8 in gymnosperms, 2-3 in flowering plants). One of these cells is a tube cell. Once the pollen grain lands on the stigma of a receptive flower (or a female cone in gymnosperms), it takes up water and germinates. Pollen germination is facilitated by hydration on the stigma, as well as by the structure and physiology of the stigma and style. Pollen can also be induced to germinate *in vitro* (in a petri dish or test tube).

During germination, the tube cell elongates into a pollen tube. In the flower, the pollen tube then grows towards the ovule where it discharges the sperm produced in the pollen grain for fertilization. The germinated pollen grain with its two sperm cells is the mature male microgametophyte of these plants.

Self-incompatibility

Since most plants carry both male and female reproductive organs in their flowers, there is a high risk of self-pollination and thus inbreeding. Some plants use the control of pollen germination as a way to prevent this self-pollination. Germination and growth of the pollen tube involve molecular signaling between stigma and pollen. In self-incompatibility in plants, the stigma of certain plants can molecularly recognize pollen from the same plant and prevent it from germinating.

Spore Germination

Germination can also refer to the emergence of cells from resting spores and the growth of sporeling hyphae or thalli from spores in fungi, algae and some plants.

Conidia are asexual reproductive spores of fungi which germinate under specific conditions. A variety of cells can be formed from the germinating conidia. The most common are germ tubes which grow and develop into hyphae. Another type of cell is a conidial anastomosis tube (CAT); these differ from germ tubes in that they are thinner, shorter, lack branches, exhibit determinate growth and home toward each other. Each cell is of a tubular shape, but the conidial anastomosis tube forms a bridge that allows fusion between conidia.

Resting Spores

In resting spores, germination that involves cracking the thick cell wall of the dormant spore. For example, in zygomycetes the thick-walled zygosporangium cracks open and the zygospore inside gives rise to the emerging sporangiophore. In slime molds, germination refers to the emergence of amoeboid cells from the hardened spore. After cracking the spore coat, further development involves cell division, but not necessarily the development of a multicellular organism (for example in the free-living amoebas of slime molds).

Ferns and Mosses

In plants such as bryophytes, ferns, and a few others, spores germinate into independent gametophytes. In the bryophytes (e.g., mosses and liverworts), spores germinate into protonemata, similar to fungal hyphae, from which the gametophyte grows. In ferns, the gametophytes are small, heart-shaped prothalli that can often be found underneath a spore-shedding adult plant.

Seedling

A seedling is a young plant sporophyte developing out of a plant embryo from a seed. Seedling development starts with germination of the seed. A typical young seedling consists of three main parts: the radicle (embryonic root), the hypocotyl (embryonic shoot), and the cotyledons (seed leaves). The two classes of flowering plants are distinguished by their numbers of seed leaves: Monocotyledons (monocots) have one blade-shaped cotyledon, whereas dicotyledons (dicots) possess two round cotyledons. Gymnosperms are more varied. For example, pine seedlings have up to eight cotyledons. The seedlings of some flowering plants have no cotyledons at all. These are said to be acotyledons.

During germination, the young plant emerges from its protective seed coat with its radicle first, followed by the cotyledons. The radicle orients towards gravity, while the hypocotyl orients away from gravity and elongates through cell expansion to push the cotyledons out of the ground.

Photomorphogenesis and Etiolation

Dicot seedlings grown in the light develop short hypocotyls and open cotyledons exposing the epicotyl. This is also referred to as photomorphogenesis. In contrast, seedlings grown in the dark develop long hypocotyls and their cotyledons remain closed around the epicotyl in an *apical hook*. This is referred to as skotomorphogenesis or etiolation. Etiolated seedlings are yellowish in color as chlorophyll synthesis and chloroplast development depend on light. They will open their cotyledons and turn green when treated with light.

In a natural situation, seedling development starts with skotomorphogenesis while the seedling is growing through the soil and attempting to reach the light as fast as possible. During this phase, the cotyledons are tightly closed and form the *apical hook* to protect the shoot apical meristem from damage while pushing through the soil. In many plants, the seed coat still covers the cotyledons for extra protection.

Upon breaking the surface and reaching the light, the seedling's developmental programme is switched to photomorphogenesis. The cotyledons open upon contact with light (splitting the seed coat open, if still present) and become green, forming the first photosynthetic organs of the young plant. Until this stage, the seedling lives off the energy reserves stored in the seed. The opening of the cotyledons exposes the shoot apical meristem and the *plumule* consisting of the first *true leaves* of the young plant.

The seedlings sense light through the light receptors phytochrome (red and far-red light) and cryptochrome (blue light). Mutations in these photo receptors and their signal transduction components lead to seedling development that is at odds with light conditions, for example seedlings that show photomorphogenesis when grown in the dark.

Seedling Growth and Maturation

Once the seedling starts to photosynthesize, it is no longer dependent on the seed's energy reserves. The apical meristems start growing and give rise to the root and shoot. The first "true" leaves expand and can often be distinguished from the round cotyledons through their species-dependent distinct shapes. While the plant is growing and developing additional leaves, the cotyledons eventually senesce and fall off. Seedling growth is also affected by mechanical stimulation, such as by wind or other forms of physical contact, through a process called thigmomorphogenesis.

CHAPTER – 5

Importance of Maize

Maize is one of the three cereals, together with rice and wheat, that make up the backbone of the world's food supply. The versatile use of maize furthermore, means that over the next decades the importance of maize will increase even further. Considering the less than impressive cob of the ancestor of maize, teosinte, this was far from a foregone conclusion and exactly how it happened is still being debated. Part of the explanation is found in the biology of maize, and in particular in how it reproduces, and how it interacts with the environment. All of these issues directly or indirectly play a part in the maize seed systems of small-scale farmers in Oaxaca, and the following chapter provides a short overview primarily targeted at readers new to maize.

Maize is one of the world's most important crops. Measured in terms of area harvested or in terms of its global average contribution to human daily calorie intake, maize ranks third after wheat and rice; however, measured in terms of total production, it is the most important cereal crop.

Maize is grown around the world from 50 degrees north to 50 degrees south; from sea level to altitudes above 3,000 masl, on flat lands and steep slopes, and in climates ranging from tropical to temperate and from semi-arid to extremely wet. In this sense, maize is today the world's most widely grown cereal, a fact that reflects its ability to adapt to a wide range of agricultural environments.

Approximately 69 per cent or 99 of the 144 million hectares of maize in the world are grown in the developing world according to FAO. Nevertheless, only about 44 per cent of the global maize harvest is produced in this part of the world. A wide gap (>5t/ha) in average maize yields/ha continues to exist between the developed world and the developing world Global maize demand is projected to increase by 50 per cent from 1995 to 2020. By 2020 maize demand in the developing world is expected to exceed the demand for both wheat and rice. In the developing world alone the demand is expected to increase almost 80 per cent. Rising incomes in certain parts of the developing world, and with that, increased consumption of meat and poultry, particularly in East and South-east Asia, is resulting in growing demand for maize as animal feed.

In other parts of the developing world maize continues to be the most important food crop and the source for more than a quarter of the average daily calorie intake per capita, for example, in Eastern and southern Africa as well as in Central America and the Caribbean. In Sub-Saharan Africa, Central America and parts of South Asia, the persistence of poverty in combination with continued population growth is expected to continue upward pressure on maize demand for human consumption. In Sub-Saharan Africa, for example, the annual maize demand is expected to double between 1995 and 2020, and in many Latin American countries the demand for food maize continues to be high.

No other crop produces so much food per unit of land or labour as maize and no other cereal crop has so many uses as maize. Maize also plays an important role in relation to global food security. This is particularly the case in Africa and Latin America, where maize makes up a significant part of the overall daily per capita calorie intake. In Zambia, Lesotho and Malawi, maize contributes more than 50 per cent of the average daily calorie intake, while in the Americas, in countries like Guatemala, Mexico, El Salvador and Honduras, maize remains the source of more than 30 per cent of the average calorie intake per capita per day.

Meanwhile, the demand for maize as livestock feed, mainly for poultry and pigs, is growing significantly, as the living standards in several developing countries, especially in Asia, is rising and the demand for meat and eggs increase.

In addition to its importance as a food crop and its value as animal feed, maize has several other diverse uses both in a rural household and in industry, Whether fresh or processed, maize can be used as food for humans, as feed for animals, as a raw material in the industrial production of starch, oil, sugar, protein, cellulose, ethylic alcohol, as construction material, for fuel, mulching, for the artisanal fabrication of handicrafts and tools.

In the industrialized world, the role of maize as human food is minimal. The major role of maize in this part of the world is as feed, mainly for cattle, pigs and poultry, and as raw material in a number of extractive industries. As researcher points out, maize is therefore a significant if indirect input in the production of meat, eggs, milk, cheese and butter, as well as in an endless list of other products. Among others researcher lists products as diverse as whiskey, chewing gum and soft drinks, toothpaste, shaving cream, shoe polish, detergents, rayon, rubber tires, explosives and embalming fluid.

The Origin and Spread of Maize

The Origin of Maize

Maize is unknown in the wild, and maize as we know it today is unable to survive without human interference. The maize cob is so tightly wrapped in the husks and the seeds so tightly compacted and attached to the cob that maize is unable to reproduce itself without the farmer's help. Even if a whole ear is buried and left to sprout, the young shoots will overcrowd each other and perish. For maize to survive on its own more than two years without human intervention would be astounding. The origin of maize has been much debated in the past, and several theories regarding its ancestry and place of origin and domestication have been proposed These often feature other members of the *Maydeae* tribe such as teosinte, the common name for a group of annual and perennial species of the genus *Zea*, and tripsacum, *Zea*'s sister genus (Doebley, 2003). Among the early theories, one argued that maize was developed from teosinte with the help of early humans. Other hypotheses held that cultivated maize was domesticated from an earlier, hypothetical 'wild maize', which had later become extinct, and that teosinte on the other hand was the result of hybridization of maize and tripsacum or, as was later suggested, from the hybridization of maize and perennial teosinte.

In addition, the extraordinary morphological and genetic diversity of maize, as well as its widespread cultivation in the Americas at the time of the conquest, lead some scientists to suggest that maize domestication had taken place independently in multiple locations.

Today, however, teosinte is widely recognized by scientists as the ancestor of maize.

Furthermore, studies using multilocus microsatelite genotyping, a technique that was unavailable until a few years ago, have produced strong indications that maize evolved from a single domestication, and that this took place approximately 9,000years ago in Southern Mexico. Moreover, the research by Matsuoka et al. clearly indicated the progenitor of maize to be *Zea parviglumis,* which is a subspecies of teosinte The evolution of maize from teosinte is highly unlikely to have taken place without human interference, and it is widely believed today, that humans were a crucial selective agent in the evolution and domestication of maize. As a result of, on the one hand favourable natural mutations and hybridization betweendifferent types of maize, and on the other hand farmers' selection for ear and grain size, as well as colour, and other kernel and plant characteristics, maize evolved from a wild plant with a small, self-sowing type of 'ear', into a highly productive plant with multi-rowed ears enclosed in a protective husk and with multiple uses.

The oldest known remains of domesticated maize were found in the Guila Naquitz cave in the Central Valleys of Oaxaca and date back approximately 6,250 years. Before Piperno and Flannery's reanalysis of the finds from Guila Naquitz, the earliest maize cobs known were thought to be from Tehuacan on the border between Puebla and Oaxaca. No crops are thought to have been domesticated in Mexico earlier than 10,000 years ago. Hence, it is estimated that maize was domesticated between 6,000 and 10,000 years ago. This is consistent with indications from molecular dating analysis, which suggests that maize was domesticated in Southern Mexico about 9,000 years ago.

The fact that the oldest archaeological maize finds are from Oaxaca, points in the direction of Oaxaca as the area of domestication of maize. However, it is not unlikely that even older maize remains may be found elsewhere in the future.

Zea parviglumis is a contemporary teosinte subspecies. It is still found in the wild between 400 and 1800 masl in the Rio Balsas region, along the western escarpment of Mexico from Nayarit to Oaxaca.Within the highlands of Southern Mexico, Oaxaca and the area of the Rio Balsas watershed on the border between the states of Michoacan and Guererro are both regarded as possible locations for maize domestication.

However, of the teosintes found today, the type most closely related to maize is found in the Rio Balsas region. This may be seen as pointing in the direction of this area as the location of maize domestication, although it should be noted that the modern distribution of teosinte populations may not be the same as during the domestication period.

Mexico is widely recognized as a centre of diversity for maize. Though ancient maize remains have been found elsewhere in the Americas, none of these are thought to predate the earliest Mexican finds. The presence of *Zea Parviglumis* in modern day Mexico, and the results of various studies using modern population genetic analysis and other advanced technologies, furthermore point convincingly to Southern Mexico as the original cradle of maize.

Numerous artefacts and other archaeological evidence testify to the importance of maize in the ancient cultures of the Americas.

At the time of the Europeans' arrival, maize was grown in large parts of the American continent. The analyses of indicate two main routes of maize's dispersal throughout the Americas. One took maize through western and northern Mexico into the south-west of the US, from where it continued to spread eastwards and north into Canada and the eastern US. Meanwhile a south-bound route went through the western and southern Statue with maize ear headdress and a maize ear in each hand. The figure's protruding lips, elliptical eye shape and ear rings are characteristic of Oaxacan funerary urns. Based on the characteristics of the maize, the piece is suspected of being post-Columbian.

Urn depicting the God Cocijo with a collar of maize ears; period Monte Alban IV (A.D. 750-1000), Museo Nacional de Antropologia 6-6758, here from Eubanks, 1999. God of Lightening and Rain, Cocijo was the most important deity in the Zapotec pantheon. "Since maize was the mainstay of pre-Columbian life and the development and survival of urban society depended on its successful production, this divinity, who controlled the elements on which the success of maize and other crops depended, was ofparamount importance".

Lowlands of Mexico into Central America and the Caribbean Islands and from there into the lowlands of South

America and finally the Andean region. In addition, archaeological evidence suggests continued contact and exchanges through time between populations of Meso- and South America, which may well have included maize. Maize continued to develop alongside pre-columbian civilizations and became one of the most important food staples, if not *the* most important, in much of pre-hispanic America. Indeed, as it has been suggested that hybridization of maize from Meso- and South America, resulting in more productive and higher yielding races better equipped for adaptation to different agro-ecological conditions may have played an important role in terms of increased food supply, which in turn may have accelerated population growth and the development of these civilizations.

On the 5 of November, 1492, two members of Columbus' crew returned from an expedition into the interior of Cuba. Among other things they reported that the natives had a kind of grain, they called 'mahiz', which tasted good and which they baked, dried and made into flour. The two crew members were probably the first Europeans to have seen the plant which has since become one of the world's most important food crops, not to mention its importance in numerous other respects - as scientists comment, "a cereal treasure of immensely greater value than the spices, which Columbus travelled so far to seek". When he returned from his first journey in 1493, Columbus brought kernels of yellow flint maize from Cuba to Spain where it was received with much interest. According to scientist, what arrived with Columbus as a botanical curiosity, became an important commercial field crop within just a hundred years, and was widely grown in Spain, Italy and southern France by the end of the 1500s.

Its high multiplication ratio and high yield potential spurred maize's spread from Europe to Asia and Africa with the explorers and traders of the 16 century. By the mid 1700s maize had established a strong foothold in west and central Africa where it had even started to displace other food crops;

it had also spread to south and south-east Asia and was a well-established crop in several of the southern Chinese provinces.

Meanwhile in North America, need led European settlers to adopt this 'Indian corn' which they regarded with a certain disdain, as a substitute for wheat. As researcher put it maize became "the bridge by which the pioneers crossed America to the Missouri", and "decade after decade, beginning in 1780, the progress of American civilization was measured by the western expansion of the corn acreage".

Maize Breeding Basics

Throughout this thesis, I refer to different types of maize populations, including landraces, creolized varieties and modern or 'improved' varieties. The term maize population can be used as a generic term for any group of maize plants under management by breeders or farmers. 'Landrace' is used to refer to "a locally grown maize population that has been the result of farmer selection and management over many generations".

An 'improved or modern variety' is a maize population that has been scientifically bred and conforms to the International Union for the Protection of New Varieties of Plants, UPOV, criteria of being distinct, uniform and stable. A creolized variety is an originally improved variety that has been under farmer management for several generations.

The term 'farmer variety' is sometimes used to refer to a crop population that a group of farmers recognize as a distinct unit, regardless of whether it is a landrace, an 'improved' or creolized variety. They may, or may not, have specific names beyond the colour of the kernel. 'Farmer variety' contrasts with the variety concept used in the context of developed country agriculture, where a 'variety' is defined as a plant grouping within a single botanical taxon of the lowest rank; this grouping can be defined by the expression of characteristics resulting from a given genotype or combination of genotypes. Additionally for a commercial variety it should be new, distinct, uniform, and stable, as according to UPOV mentioned above.

Open Pollinated

In self-pollinating crops, for example wheat and rice, pollination of the ovules of each individual plant happens with pollen from the same plant. The genetic make-up of the crop population remains largely unchanged from one generation to the next. However, maize is an open-pollinated crop. This means that the ovules of each plant are largely pollinated by pollen from other maize plants, or, put in a different way, that the male and female heritage is contributed by two different plants. Under natural circumstances maize reproduction therefore entails a high degree of exchange of genetic material between plants.

When the silks of a maize plant are fertilized by pollen from the same plant, scientists refer to the resulting kernels as *inbred*. Inbreeding decreases genetic variability, thereby increasing the uniformity of the maize in this case. However, inbreeding also increases the frequency of deleterious mutations, which can lead to a decline in plant vigour in species,like maize, that are normally open-pollinated. This phenome *Maize* non is also called inbreeding depression. According to agricultural scientists, after three generations of systematic, targeted inbreeding, maize will yield only half as much as usual, though it will be very uniform. A similar effect sometimes occurs in farmers' fields, though normally over a much longer time span.

If the farmer, who selects and saves seed from his/her own maize harvest year after year, selects all the seed from a very limited number of cobs, the genetic variation of the seed lot may eventually become so limited that the frequency of deleterious mutations will increase and inbreeding depression will be the result. Mexican small-scale farmers will sometimes refer to this phenomenon by saying that the maize has become tired (*cansado*).

While maize self-pollination or inbreeding tends to produce offspring that underperform their parents, the crossing of genetically different maize plants tends to produce offspring that perform better than their parents. This phenomenon is known as *hybrid vigour* or heterosis. In their own way farmers sometimes make use of this phenomenon. When Mexican smallscale farmers consider that their maize has become 'tired', they will sometimes deliberately mix their maize with another kind of maize in order to make their own maize 'stronger' (*para reforzar el maíz*).

In principle the term hybrid simply refers to an animal or a plant produced from genetically distinct parents. However, maize scientists have combined the mechanisms of both inbreeding and hybrid vigour in the creation of what has come to be known as *hybrid maize*. The use of inbreeding serves to limit the genetic variability and enhance the homogeneity of lines used as parents;and the c rossing of genetically distinct parents are used to achieve hybrid vigour. Many different types of hybrid maize exists; as an example, a singlecross hybrid is produced by crossing two distinct inbred parents: Inbred A × inbred B = single-cross hybrid AB.

The first generation of a hybrid will exhibit more vigorous growth, yield or disease resistance than either of its parents. However, the hybrid vigour effect tends to decline in subsequent generations. Though the degree of this decline varies between the different types of hybrids, single-cross hybrids are often highly unstable and may exhibit yield declines of 25-40 per cent or more already in the second generation. This may not prove a problem in areas where a well-developed formal seed sector exists, and farmers are able to buy fresh commercial seed every year. However, yield stability is an important issue in relation to hybrid maize seed in areas where farmers do not have reliable access to seed supply or are accustomed to selecting and recycling seed from their previous harvest.

Another popular strategy for the development of improved maize varieties consists of routinely crossing genetically diverse maize types in order to develop maize populations, which are then improved through recurrent selection.

This category of improved maize is normally referred to as OPVs or *open-pollinated varieties*. According to the CIMMYT Maize Programme an OPV can be defined as an assemblage of phenotypes that is different, relatively uniform and stable. As mentioned above, all maize is naturally open pollinated. However, the use of the term OPV refers to the fact that seed is produced by open (uncontrolled) pollination, as opposed to hybrid varietieswhich require controlled pollination.

Modern hybrid maize demonstrates a yield advantage in comparison to improved OPVs. However, while studies have shown best hybrids to be superior over best OPVs by an average of 15-20 per cent, improved OPVs do not show the dramatic declines in yield characteristic of hybrids, in subsequent generations. For example, the effect of planting recycled seed to be negligible for OPVs, severe for hybrids (>30%) and intermediate for topcross hybrids (approximately 16%).

OPVs have an important role in maize agriculture in developing countries. Compared to hybrid maize, improved OPVs are easier to develop and their seed production is simpler and relatively inexpensive. Furthermore, farmers can recycle the seed of OPVs for 3-4 years with only negligible to minimal yield declines. Thus, instead of buying new seed every year, it is only necessary to buy new seed every 3-4 years, a fact that significantly reduces farmers' dependence on external seed sources. Furthermore, as management and input requirements for OPVs are similar to those of many local landraces used by poor maize farmers, farmer-to-farmer seed flow is relatively uncomplicated.

Genotype-by-environment Interaction

Environmental factors play an important role in crop performance; however, some crops respond more strongly than others across different environments.

Maize exhibits what plant breeders call a high *genotype-by-environment interaction* or G × E, meaning that its' performance across different agro-ecological environments depends on its specific genetic make-up. In other words, a genotype, that is, the specific genetic constitution of a certain maize 'variety', which performs well in one environment, may not do so in another. The ability to perform under extremely diverse growing conditions reflects the impressive morphological and genetic diversity in maize, which enables this crop to adapt to a wide range of environments. At the same time, though, maize's genotype-environment sensitivity also means that, often, a maize 'variety' that is well adapted to a specific growing environment will not perform satisfactorily if introduced into a markedly different agro-ecological context.

A process of adaptation is sometimes possible which can mitigate this, for example, through farmers' selection or what breeders call adaptive breeding. However, the essence of maize's high genotype-by-environment interaction is that different maize 'varieties' are appropriate and will perform well in different agro-ecological environments. For formal maize breeding purposes this also means that maize breeding efforts must be targeted carefully to relatively specific agro-ecological conditions. For example, the hybrid maize varieties that are popular in the American Midwest are not appropriate in the tropics – in fact, they may not even be able to produce viable seed. This has important implications for farmers, who must make sure that the varieties they plant are appropriate for the particular agro-ecological conditions present on the farm.

Maize's scientific name is *Zea mays* L. Like all the major cereals, it is a grass. In botanical terms, maize forms part of the *Gramineae* family, within which it belongs to the *Maydeae* tribe.

A mature maize plant normally has a single dominant stalk. The stalk has between 8 and 20 nodes from each of which a leaf emerges on alternate sides of the stalk. The part between the nodes is called the internode and is where growth takes place. The roots of maize are thestrongest of all annual crop plants. The main roots may penetrate as much as 1.5 – 1.8 meter into the ground and 0.9 – 1.2 meter sideways. In addition maize often features brace roots beginning 2-3 nodes above the ground.

While some types of maize barely reach a maximum height of 1 meter, others grow to more than 5 times this height. At the top the stalk ends in a tassel with 5-20 branches, each with hundreds of little spikelets, which are the male flowers of the maize plant. From nodes along the stem several ear shoots may develop, each covered by a protective layer of husk leaves. While most of the ear shoots degenerate, one or two will continue to develop into the female inflorescence of the maize plant. The maize plants' ability to convert sunlight, water, air and soil into biomass is extraordinary. In about 3 months a single maize seed can develop into a plant more than 5 meters tall, carrying more than 1000 seeds.

When flowering time approaches, a tuft of silks will protrude from the tip of the ear. Each silk is connected to an ovule on the maize cob, and each ovule is a potential maize kernel. Ovules and silks make up the female element of the maize plant. Each spikelet on the tassel contains a number of pollen sacs, also called anthers.

When these ripen they begin to shed pollen - the male element of the maize plant. The moment a pollen grain lands on a silk, it starts to travel down through the silk for 20-25 cm to the ovule, where the pollinization is completed.can vary considerably, and depends, in part, on the number of rows of kernels on the cob. Some cobs have only 8 rows, while others can have up to 30 rows. Similarly, maize ears come in different sizes ranging from 7.5 – 40 cm long.

The shape of maize kernels depends on the type of maize in question. Dented maize has wrinkled or indented kernels; flintmaize has smooth kernels; and floury maize has smooth – slightly dented kernels.

Maize kernels can be different colours; including white, yellow, black and red, and for each of these different nuances may apply. Finally, some maize is of mixed colour, that is, produce ears with kernels of 2-4 different colours, for example, white-and-black, or white-black-and-yellow.

Only in yellow maize does the pigment that gives the kernel its particular colour reside in the endosperm; in black/ blue, red and white maize the pigmentation is limited to a thin layer just below the pericarp and covering the endosperm. The oblong centre of the maize kernel is the germ, that is, the dormant seedling from which a new maize plant will grow. It is surrounded by the endosperm, a body of starch which serves as nutrition for the germinating seedling. The kernel is covered by a thin membrane called the pericarp, and is attachedto the cob by the pedicel. On average a maize kernel contains 72 per cent starch, 10 per cent protein, 3 per cent sugar, 4.8 per cent oil, 8.5 per cent fibre and 1.7 per cent ash, of which the oil is contained in the germ, while the rest are in the surrounding endosperm.

CHAPTER – 6

Local Seed Practices

Local seed practices are often referred to as making up or being part of informal seed systems. This implicitly suggests that they make up some sort of system and that it should be possible to document this system in relatively clear terms. In the study in Oaxaca a wide range of disciplines and methodologies were involved in efforts to document many different aspects of local maize seed practices, ranging from participant observation, structured or semi-structuredsurveys of socio-economic factors and seed practices, to using molecular markers to analyse maize diversity in the study area. This multitude of disciplines and approaches gave rise to many stimulating discussions on what is the local seed system, and how we can describe it.

However, often we had the feeling that the more we learned, the less able we were to describe it in words, drawings, schemas, and likewise the increased knowledge questioned the notion of seeing it as a system. This chapter attempts to describe local seed practices in the study area. However, I also argue that doing this in a linguistic medium (i.e. writing), and attempting to use precise terminology can at best be very partial, and that the limited verbalization should be an important consideration when choosing methodologies for studying seed practices. This argument will be built on theories of local knowledge and in particular on the cognitive aspects of knowledge.

The discussion of seed practices includes the following elements:

- A local knowledge perspective
- Concepts of grain, seed, and variety
- Varietal choice
- Choice of seed source
- On-farm seed management practices
- Moral dimensions of seed management

Local Knowledge

Local knowledge is a resource and an area of great relevance both for research and for applied development. In relation to local knowledge, the two are often closely linked or seem to flow together and it can be difficult to establish a clear line between them. Indeed, local knowledge is a field which brings together the academic and the practical. In this section follow this line of thinking. When using examples from both development and research, the attention paid to separating the two will therefore be limited.

Local knowledge is introduced from a more theoretical perspective, addressing issues related to terminology and relevance of local knowledge, ownership, as well as the negotiation and communication of local knowledge. A presentation and discussion of findings regarding farmers seed concepts and practices in the study area follows.

Scientists offers a broad definition of knowledge as "what a person employs to interpret and act on the world", or, "all the ways of understanding that we use to make up our experienced, grasped reality". As Barth subsequently notes, different people's stock of knowledge varies notably and is highly influenced by a variety of factors, such as ethnographic, social, educational and developmental diversity.

It is generally in order to emphasize one or several of such contextual factors, that some authors refer to 'indigenous knowledge'; 'local knowledge'; 'cultural knowledge'; or 'traditional knowledge'.

Though these terms should not be considered as synonymous, and while no standard definition of local or indigenous knowledge exists, it is generally understood as referring to theories, beliefs, practices and technologies, which are distinct from those usually associated with what is known as 'Western' or 'conventional' scientific knowledge.

However, the appropriateness of each of these various terms, and the meanings with which each author invests them (e.g. whether they are regarded politically correct or not), has been subject to much debate, though no clear agreement has apparently been reached. For example, for some, 'traditional' knowledge invokes an image of something static, thereby ignoring people's creative experimentation and innovation. Similarly, theterms 'folk knowledge' or 'folk science' have been considered to be pejorative in comparison with modern science or knowledge.

The view informing the work presented here is an understanding of knowledge as complex, fragmented, continuously evolving and subject to negotiation. 'Local knowledge' here, because the ideas and practices of farmers in the Central Valleys of Oaxaca regarding maize and maize farming are very much influenced by factors related to the local socio-cultural and agro-ecological context.

The Relvance of Local Knowledge in Research and Development

After a chapter in its history, which featured a series of quite problematic attempts to establish a field of practical application of anthropology, including some unfortunate association with colonialism, most anthropologists stayed close to the discipline's 'safer', academic side for many years. The 'pure' from the 'practical', or the 'academic' from the 'applied', has influenced the field of anthropology over several decades, causing a certain ambivalence in relation to the fields of development and local knowledge.

However, as participatory approaches have become part of mainstream development over the last decades, so the awareness of local people's knowledge and its potential as a resource for research and development has increased significantly.

Appreciating and drawing on local knowledge and practices when planning and implementing development interventions and research can help make these initiatives more useful and sympathetic to local contexts and contribute greatly to their chances ofachieving longer term sustainability.

Hence, the realization among large segments of the development community of the value of drawing on and incorporating local knowledge, has, in recent times, generated a remarkable increase in research on various forms of local knowledge and on knowledge processes more generally. As Sillitoe expresses it, this development provides a much needed opportunity within anthropology to bring the 'academic' and the 'applied' closer together, since it presents "a better opportunity to show our mettle than ever before".

Researcher identifies five areas where applied local knowledge research is likely to be relevant. Firstly, he suggests, in relation to the introduction of new technologies, that local knowledge research can be useful in order to increase the relevance and adaptation of new technology to local cultural and agroecological contexts. Secondly, he sees a role for local knowledge research inrelation to initiatives that explore the potential of developing local solutions to specific problems, based on local people's own resources and practices.

Thirdly, the that applied local knowledge research also has a role to play in what he calls 'the furthering of cultural diffusion'. That is, in assessing the relevance of introducing knowledge and practices from one context to another where they may also be useful for local problem-solving. Fourthly, Sillitoe mentions the use of research for identifying local elements and practices which may have a commercial potential, such as bio-prospecting.

Finally, the use of local knowledge research for supporting, what he calls 'alternative development'. That is, development initiatives which are not necessarily part of 'conventional' development programmes which often focus on technical matters, but address instead political issues or consider alternative perspectives, such as interaction between humans and nature, and local people's own visions of their futures.

Another interesting contribution on knowledge processes on the valuation of local knowledge. He argues that, though participatory approaches are now very much part of development 'vocabulary' and recognition of the value of local knowledge has grown significantly, meaningful attempts to incorporate local knowledge into rural development initiatives remain weak. In Shepherd's opinion, agricultural development remains heavily influenced by the narrative of deficiency in local livelihoods and indigenous knowledge.

He goes on to state that by virtue of its foundation in 'modern' science, development expertise lays claim to an objective assessment of local problems. Indeed, at times, local knowledge and practices are even regarded as "part and parcel of the problem of low productivity, gender inequality, poverty, etcetera, in the expectation that these adversities will be alleviated given the right technology and expertise".

According to Shepherd, such narratives of deficiency that permeate development policy and practice seriously constrain the appreciation of the importance of culture and local knowledge for development and conservation. For this to change, it is necessary to shift away from positivist approaches to knowledge still inherent in orthodox rural development circles, although, it remains unclear to what degree Shepherd argues for a complete rejection of 'scientific' knowledge in relation to development.

Making indigenous knowledge accessible to other scientists and relevant to their research raises considerable methodological problems which should not be under-estimated. Drawing an example from the highlands of New Guinea, the complex interweaving of local agricultural production with a diversity of socio-cultural factors, including labour considerations, social relations, gender ideology, sexuality and bodily substances. From a local perspective, specific development problems should not be understood as isolated constraints, but as involving multiple factors from both natural and socio-cultural realms.

However, taking the socio-cultural embeddedness too far, thus implying that some ethnographic accounts may strike scientists as "esoteric records which they are unable to relate to their work". In the end, this may put off those very scientists that one needs to engage. Hence, in agreement with Warren (1989), he stresses the importance of ensuring that indigenous knowledge is conveyed to scientists in such a way that they can appreciate its relevance.

Yet, despite the realization and growing appreciation of the value and significance of local knowledge, studies have also shown that local knowledge can be imprecise, incomplete or mistaken. Indeed, several authors have stressed the need to be careful not to romanticize or falsely glamorise local knowledge.

As noted by several writers, efforts to demonstrate the value of local knowledge and increase its recognition and incorporation into research and development have been suspected of trying to undermine the scientific establishment and of promoting 'second-best' solutions to local problems, thereby depriving people of access to the 'best' and newest technologies. However, as Sillitoe asserts, the push for increased understanding and use of local know ledge is not about undermining science. In fact, it is generally agreed thascience has a lot to offer farmers. The debate is less about this, and more about how to make the outcomes of scientific research and knowledge production more effective, accessible and relevant to people in their local contexts.

According to scientist, the objective of indigenous knowledge research is to create dynamic linkages between local people's perspectives and practices and those of researchers and development professionals, in order to contribute over the long term to positive change for local people via the promotion of culturally appropriate and environmentally sustainable adaptations.

If indigenous knowledge is to be successful in linking local people's perceptions and aspirations, and scientific technocrats' research agendas, then it is necessary to promote facilitatory modalities which allow for the complementary combination of anthropological skills on one hand, and technical and scientific knowledge on the other. *Issues regarding the ownership of local knowledge*

Local knowledge research has many links to ethnobiology, which in turn has roots in the exploration of 'useful' flora and fauna of potential economic interest. Ethnobiology has since found a role in the development debate and, to a large degree, has become "absorbed into the rhetoric of 'indigenous knowledge' and 'indigenous rights' along with other disciplines.

Not surprisingly, with the recognition of the value of local knowledge and its potentialprospects for scientific or economic gain, the issue of its study and use has become highly politicised and, increasingly, controversies over rights and ownership have arisen. The issues in question typically concern the commercial exploitation of biodiversity and local knowledge, often referred to as 'bioprospecting', or 'biopiracy', and, most notably focusing upon the use of ethnobotany by the pharmaceutical industries.

This debate concerning the ownership of local knowledge has spread and now involves a wide range of aspects of biodiversity, including crop genetic resources and related local knowledge. Meanwhile, despite the conflicts and unresolved questions regarding intellectual property rights of farmers and indigenous peoples, ethnobiology and local knowledge research are contributing to the development of guidelines for responsible research and use of these resources for the benefit of both national and commercial interests. At the same time, these initiatives have significantly contributed to the promotion of participatory approaches in research and development, as well as the protection of farmers' and indigenous people's rights, although much still remains to be done in this regard.

These problems relating to the use of genetic resources and local knowledge *vis-à-vis* local people's rights to their cultural heritage, and opportunities for useful and profitable, exploitation of these resources, constitute a cause of unease for many researchers.

Active involvement in these matters can be controversial. Some find it paternalistic and interfering, while others consider it a responsibility that cannot be ignored. The five areas where local knowledge research could play an important role have different degrees of 'purity/applicability'; two of them approach this challenge from opposite sides - the commercial use of knowledge, versus support for alternative development - however, all of them are problematic.

The Negotiation of Local Knowledge

Much of the earlier literature on knowledge was based on the assumption that knowledge is something unitary and systematized critical overviews. But over the last decades this has begun to change. It is now broadly accepted that knowledge is not uniform and evenly distributed among specific populations. Gender, age group, ethnicity, religion, occupation and training, for example, often mark differences in people's stocks of knowledge and perspectives, even among those who live and work under seemingly similar circumstances.

Likewise, the way that different people and groups interpret shared knowledge will vary according to their respective interests. Nevertheless, as researchers point out, losing oneself in the details of these differencesruns the risk of overlooking other levels of broadly shared understandings.

It may also result in neglecting the negotiations, manoeuvrings andalliances that take place between different social groups. However, in many contexts knowledge remains fragmentary and diffuse, and dynamic and negotiated, since it emerges as an "outcome of the interactions, negotiations, interfaces and accommodations that take place between different actors and their lifeworlds". To fully grasp the nature of this requires an exploration of the processes by which knowledge becomes part of particular practices.

Studies of the social aspects of knowledge have also focused on issues relating to power: That is, on how power influences what is considered knowledge and how discourses on knowledge reproduce power relations. Interface analysis has been used in a series of studies of the multilayered and contested nature of knowledge along with local people's negotiations over resources, meanings and control, for example, with government officials or representatives from private companies.

However, these battles do not belong only to development practitioners. The negotiations of meanings and discourses take place within and among various groups of actors, thus engaging both local people, social activists, extensionists and other professionals, as well as policy makers, donors and researchers.

Often these actors are involved in multiple 'projects' at the same time. Writing of an agro-biodiversity project in Peru, Shepherd reflects on the divisions and negotiations among the farmers themselves, which run parallel to the discourses of various local development organizations. He notes that "The desires and needs of campesinos, however, presented a much more ambiguous picture than the parameters of discourse and counter-discourse would have us believe. There were no stable or unchanging alliances".

For example, in order to avoid being considered shifting cultivators,which is illegal, they often omit certain relevant details or share cultural information selectively by emphasizing the gathering of non-timber-forestproducts while omitting or down-playing their slash-and-burn activities.

In a similar manner, an 'idealised' version of the Batak as hunter-gatherers is sometimes used by conservationist groups, despite the fact that shifting cultivation is an important Batak practice. Novellino goes on to argue that the use of miscommunication constitutes a form of negotiation: That is, it creativelyuses ambiguity, omission, deception and seduction to avoid conflicts, or for stalling a process.

Novellino reflects critically on the use of formal questionnaires as an example of miscommunication between Batak and external experts. Batak interviewees were asked to locate themselves according to categories that do not exist in their own language and thus were found meaningless. Similarly, Batak community members were asked to indicate which of three possibilities were their most urgent local needs: drinking water, irrigation or electrification, when none were recognized as 'needs'. As Novellino remarks, interviewees had no option but to reply to wrong questions with wrong answers.

Another example relates to the confession of local knowledge. This refers to situations where the development professional first makes Batak 'confess' their local knowledge, for example, by pretending to be genuinely interested in learning about their ways, only to follow this up by 'reproaching' the confessant for his unsustainable practices and suggesting a 'better' alternative in the form of imported agro-forestry practices. The more they talk (orare forced to talk), 'the more science knows [and] the one who listens and interprets becomes a master of the truth'.

As should now be clear, the field of local knowledge and development carries with it certain inevitable political dimensions. Local knowledge is closely linked to the wider acceptance and incorporation of participatory approaches and to the recognition of the advantages of technologies that are accessible, relevant and effective to people in their particular socio-culturaland agro-ecological settings.

However, the problem for authorities and decision makers is that they both need and fear people's participation . While the acceptance and support of the population is necessary, too much participation and involvement from 'beneficiaries' is difficult to control, and may threaten power relationships at all levels, whether local regional, national and international. This is undoubtedly one of the major constraints on conducting research on local knowledge processes aimed at achieving more equitable and effective development interventions.

Challenges in the Communication of Local Knowledge

Knowledge can be articulated in many different and complex forms. However, both in the literature as well as in the course of social life, a strong emphasis is placed on the use of language for communicating and learning about knowledge. The assumption that language is the principal means of knowledge communication has led to a strong focus on verbalized knowledge, which, in turn, makes it easy to overlook other forms. Indeed, one could say that it appears that knowledge only comes into existence once it has been expressed in words, whether verbal or written.

In anthropology the importance of drawing on cognitive theories of knowledge has been convincingly argued by the scientists, but they stress the limitations of relying too much on linguistic models of knowledge. The argument proceeds as follows:

Thinking, or the mind-brain relation, should not be modelled according to a 'sentence-logic'. Rather, it should be based on concepts which are formed through experience and practice in the external world. The concepts in our minds do not correspond to specific definitions, but are provisional, and are gradually being constituted by life experiences that lead to acquiring the particular concept.

In fact, much knowledge is non-linguistic, as is the case with embodied, performative knowledge, and much knowledge is acquired by non-linguistic processes. Many daily practical tasks or skills relating to particular trades are learned without receiving verbal instructions.

Reflecting on the limitations of written language, Hunn comments on the ways children in local communities come to know hundreds of plants and animals and associate names in their native language with them. This process involves various sensory modalities and "powerful social contexts, [and learning] from their parents, elders, and peers, though typically without formal instruction. Similarly, much practical knowledge eludes being rendered into language, and is therefore lost in descriptions.

Under some circumstances non-linguistic knowledge can be fixed into language, but this implies a transformation and not merely a translation of the knowledge. The issue of translation/transformation between verbalized and performative knowledge is very real. We could simply not carry out our most practical tasks such as driving a car, or make decisions about which fallow constitutes 'a good swidden', if we were thinking about them verbally.

However, he also points out that the transformation process may be beneficial in the sense that going back and forth between verbalized and performative knowledge may increase the knowledge in both areas.

Knowledge blocks can be strung together into increasingly complex bodies of knowledge. This is illustrated by scientist when he describes, how the building worker apprentice gradually moves on to constructing increasingly complex parts of the building. However, he also underlines that 'performative' knowledge does not share the grammatical and syntax rules that characterize verbal knowledge.

The ways that elements of knowledge within a particular knowledge domain can be combined, can vary from one domain to another, and the way performative knowledge is combined is different from that of verbalized knowledge. This implies, for example,that it is problematic to transform each element of a complex performance into an equivalent verbal representation, and then recreate the complex process from the verbal pieces according to verbal rules.

Researcher distinguishes between 'propositional' and 'performative' knowledge, or, as he also puts it, between *knowing that* and *knowing how*. Using his own experience as a building worker in Yemen, he discusses the differences between the knowledge of brick making on one hand, as theoretical or analytical knowledge gained, for example, from observing others making bricks and having the different steps in the process explained to him; and on the other hand, knowledge of how actually to make bricks, which is acquired and internalized or embodied through practice. Marchand reflects on the carving of bricks of the type 'x'.

The initial theory, or *knowing that*, that (awkwardly) guided my first attempts at carving 'x's (in co-ordination with what my body already 'knew' in terms of positioning and performance) was succeeded by a skilled and efficient performance, or *knowing how*. Retrospectively, it was apparent that this *knowing how* had likewise modified my 'conscious' *thinking about* how to make'x's, and that the two may be considered to be in dialectical relation with one another via an interface mechanism which selectively interprets information between them.

In addition to the challenge of 'translating' performative or tacit knowledge into language, the way we understand the world and interpret new knowledge is heavily influenced by what we already know, that is, by one's current stock of knowledge. This means that it is not possible to isolate 'a piece of knowledge'. In many cases one must possess a particular knowledge background in order to make sense of it.

Thus, different people with different stocks of knowledge (e.g. a city dweller compared to a scientist or a local farmer) will absorb and interpret new information in different ways. This adds to the challenge of researching local knowledge. It can be difficult - and inevitably involves additional 'transformation'- to communicate, for example, local agricultural knowledge to an urban and/or academic audience, or to communicate plant breeders' knowledge to a social scientist audience and vice versa.

Seed Concepts

From a biological perspective, any healthy maize kernel can serve as either seed or grain for consumption. Yet, both farmers and plant breeders tend to distinguish between them. Within the realm of formal crop improvement, certain criteria generally exist which define the category 'seed'.

These criteria are normally subject to formal regulation and implementation and generally include specific procedures for seed production and certification, as well ascertain minimum quality standards (e.g. regarding moisture content, germination rates and varietal purity).

Farmers in the study area may distinguish kernels as *seed* for planting or as *grain* for consumption or sale: a practice that has also been reported fromother parts of Mexico and which is *Local maize seed knowledge and practices* confirmed by this research. Smallholders in the Central Valleys of Oaxaca often refer to maize kernels in the general sense as *grano* (grain) or *maíz* (maize) without specifying its intended use. 'Grain' can be used for human consumption, animal feed, or sale.

It has not (yet) been classified according to its intended use. Its destiny is, therefore, not unequivocal. By contrast, once 'seed' has been selected it is destined specifically for planting, and, in most cases,treated in a different manner. 'Seed' represents a portion of the kernels from the farmers' harvest that has been selected as such, based on a set of criteria, according to which farmers decide from which ears to select the kernels to be used as seed, as well as which specific kernels on these ears to define as seed.

Hence, maize seed is maize kernels that have been selected as possessing certain traits associated with a high potential for producing good parent plants capable of expressing certain favoured traits. Once redefined as seed, the value of these kernels also changes. Like any valuable object or good, farmers safeguard their seed and store it in the best possible conditions, often separated from the rest of the maize.

These price differentials between seed and grain contrasts with a review of studies in Africa showing that the price charged for seed is often the same as that for grain, while in more market-oriented agriculture, seed producingfarmers are able to charge a premium. In the communitiesof the Central Valleys, the price differentials are general and not associated with a group of particular farmers (e.g., seed producers), suggesting that farmers value the general ability to select seed and the additional care taken when storing it.

In spite of the seemingly clear distinction between seed and grain, farmers may sometimes use grain as seed. This occurs mainly when farmers try out other kinds of maize; or during circumstances when it is difficult to obtain seed, for example, due to lack of resources; or to make up for the lack of just a small part of the seed needed (i.e. partial seed loss). Under these circumstances, a farmer may decide to acquire grain rather than seed, and subsequently select seed from this. However, as grain is generally managed lessrigorously than seed, this procedure can entail additional risks with regard to seed quality.

Camilo's wife Gregoria sometimes takes orders for hand-made tortillas. In some cases the person who places the order will bring her a particular kind of maize with which to make the *nixtamal*. Gregoria recalls one such occasion when she received an order for tortillas and the client brought her a bucketful of beautiful black maize fromwhich she wanted the tortillas made.

The Definition of a Variety

The concept of a 'variety' as understood in the context of industrialized agriculture and as defined by the UPOV is different from the way farmers in the study area use it. When the smallholder farmers in Oaxaca talk about different maize varieties, in most cases they simply mean different kinds of maize (i.e. different crop populations that they recognize as distinct). This may include landraces as well as creolised and modern varieties and mixturesof these.

Farmers distinctions between different kinds of maize may be based on any number and kind of characteristics of the particular maize populations in question, such as the colour of the maize kernels, their shape or the shape of the ear, the characteristics of the cobs or the husks or any other part of the plants, the length of their growing cycle or their agro-ecological adaptation.

Nevertheless, in many cases farmers also leave room for considerable variation within a 'variety'. For the outsider this can cause confusion: maize which looks the same to the outsider may be referred to as distinct varieties by the farmer. On the other hand, on several occasions the farmer would laugh, saying No! That's the same variety! referring to what believed to be ears of different kinds of maize. In addition, the farmer concept of 'variety' appears to be flexible, and at times the difference between one variety and another can be quite 'fuzzy', depending on the circumstances. Phrases such as "Those two are the same, only, they're different or No, that one is different, but it's the same seemed frequent during the fieldwork.

While farmers in the Central Valleys of Oaxaca distinguish between different 'varieties' of maize, they often do not have specific names for them beyond, for example, the colour of the kernel. A farmer may plant two varieties of white maize.

He or she may recognize and manage them as different, but not have a specific name for each of them, besides calling them both whites (blancos), adding other information to distinguish between them when needed. Don Fausto and Doña Clara (Albarradas), for example, have three kinds of white maize, which they refer to as criollo blanco (white landrace), blanco acriollado (creolized white) and criollo blanco de olote morado (white landrace with purple cob).

Another example is Tiburcio (Albarradas) who grows two white landraces, referring to them as *criollo blanco de 3 meses* (white landrace of three months) and *criollo blanco de totomoxtle morado* (white landrace with purple husk).

Occasionally maize with a particular characteristic will be recognized and referred to in a particular way by various farmers. For instance, Don Juan (San Lorenzo Albarradas) grows three different white maize landraces. He refers to two of them simply as *criollo blanco* (white landrace) and *criollo blanco de tierra fría* (white landrace of cold land, meaning cold climate) respectively. The third is characterised by its 'pointy' or 'spiky' kernels. This type of maize is referred to by Don Juan and other farmers in the community as '*maíz piña*' (pineapple maize).

The Practices of Mixing and Complementing Seed

It should be noted that, although farmers select their own seed year after year, they may also, occasionally, substitute entirely, complement, or mix their own seed with seed from other sources. Initially a farmer might state.

However, further conversation may reveal that on one or more occasions the seed was complemented or mixed with other maize seed. With regard to the study communities, these practices have also been noted and similar practices are reported from other regions in Mexico. Over time, these and other management practices (e.g. how the farmer selects seed, aswell as naturally occurring pollen flow from other farmers' maize fields), may well change the genetic make-up of his/her maize.

Farmers sometimes replace their maize seed, partially or completely, with seed from other sources than their own harvest. For example, they do this in the case of shortfall due to a poor harvest, or storage pests or, alternatively, for the purpose of experimentation (e.g. trying out other types of maize) or in order to use seed of other kinds of maize as a tool to deliberately influence orchange the characteristics of a particular type of maize.

The replacement seed can be from farmer or modern varieties or any combination of the two, and it can be acquired from a number of different sources, including other farmers, commercial seed sector stockists, local market sellers, or organizations.

Seed replacement can be total, meaning a complete replacement of the seed of a particular variety, by a new seed lot of the same or a different variety (e.g. in the case where the farmer loses all the seed of a particular variety and therefore needs to replace it; or where the farmer decides to acquire 'fresh' seed as recommended for many modern commercial varieties). However, seed replacement can also be partial. This is when the farmer only replaces part of the seed lot with seed from other sources (e.g. because only part of the seed lot was destroyed by storage pests) and the need for additional seed was just to 'complete' the amount of planting material needed. The partial replacement can also be for the purpose of testing another kind of maize; or for the purpose of deliberately influencing or changing the characteristics of the farmer's own maize by mixing or crossing it with another kind of maize. Examples of these different instances of seed replacement include:

Partial seed replacement to make up for partial seed loss during storage.

For more than 25 years Don Heriberto (Huitzo) has grown the same white maize his father gave him when he started to farm on his own.

Two years ago he found himself short of seed and in order to finish the planting he had to complement it with seed of other white maize, which he bought from two other farmers.

Partial Change in Order to Try Out Another Kind of Maize, Followed by Mixing.

Elpidio and Natalia (Albarradas) have grown different types of maize over the years. For the past 15 years they have planted a *pinto* which they acquired locally from the father of a friend. Elpidio works part time in a brick making plant (kiln) in Tlacolula.

A couple of years ago, at the market in Tlacolula, he saw a *belatove* maize (red maize) which he liked a lot, and so he bought 1 kg with the intention of planting it to try it out. The first year they planted it separately and it performed well. They harvested it together with the pinto maize and took seed from both, but mixed them, because they liked them both. Since then they have continued with the mix of *pinto* and *belatove.*

Total seed change, later followed by partial seed replacement and mixing with the purpose of deliberately altering the characteristics of the maize in question.

In a bad year when the maize harvest failed, Benito and Hipolita (Mazaltepec) lost the seed they had used until then. At the market in Oaxaca they saw a maize, which was 'very clean and had big kernels', and they decided to use this as seed for the following planting (total seed change to replace previous maize). The maizeperformed well and they liked the grain, but found the ears to have very big cobs. After some years, therefore, they mixed the seed with seed of another type of white maize in order to get a maize with a slimmer cob.

Revisiting the original data from the CIMMYT-INIFAP 1998 baseline study in the 6 study communities, Table 6.1 shows the frequencies of complete or partial seed change in relation to the number of maize seed lots registered in each of the communities in the baseline study.

Though the numbers and percentages vary from one community to another, it is noticeable that on average 49 per cent of all seed lots had never been changed, while an average of 51 per cent had been subject to either partial or complete change in the past.

For each of their different kinds of maize, farmers were asked whether they did partial or complete seed changes. Overall, 28 per cent of the different kinds of maize grown by the farmers who participated in the baseline study (240 households), had been subject to complete seed change at some stage, while in San Lorenzo Albarradas the number was as high as 50 per cent.

Meanwhile, the incidence of complete seed change carried out frequently is between 0 and 2 per cent in all study communities except for San Pablo Huitzo where it is 12 per cent or more than 10 times as high as in the other study communities. In San Pablo Huitzo there is more use of hybrid varieties and also of using maize for silage, both of which may explain in part this difference.

As for partial seed change, an average of 32 per cent of the different kinds of maize grown by the households that participated in the baseline study, had been subject to partial seed replacement in the past . The highest inci *Small holder seed practices* 130 dence of partial seed replacement (61%) was found among the participantsfrom Santa Ana Zegache, whereas the lowest (5%) was in San Pablo Huitzo. The participants in the baseline study were also asked why they would carry out either partial or total seed change. On average, 96 per cent of all *complete* seed replacements were carried out in order to replace seed, and not a single incidence was reported in which complete seed change had been done in order to try out a new kind of germplasm.

An average of 59 per cent of the *partial* seedreplacements were carried out in order to test another kind of maize or reduce the risk of testing other types of maize, and the rest of the cases of partial seed change (41%) were due to partial seed loss.

Farmers generally clearly differentiate between which part of their maize they consider seed, and which part is grain. Seed is managed with more care than grain, which also is reflected in a higher value when selling it, though this added value only applies if the receiver recognizes it as seed. The distinction between grain and seed is, however, not rigid or static, and, depending on the circumstances, a farmer may decide to use what was initially considered grain as seed, just as, for example, unused seed may revert to be used as grain.

The concept of seed is, therefore, dynamic and negotiable, depending on the circumstances, though a farmer in any given moment will have a clear idea as to whether a given bag of maize kernels contains seed or grain.

The formal seed sector concept of maize variety is that of a maize population with particular genetic characteristics, which is distinct, uniform and stable. If the genetic makeup changes, then, by definition, it is no longer that variety. Though farmers use the term variety [*variedad*], theirs is a very different concept, which is much more flexible and dynamic than the formal seed sector variety concept. One kind of maize may be mixed with another.

If the flowering coincides, this effectively means they will cross, and the resulting germplasm will be a mixture of the two. However, the farmer may not necessarily regard this as another variety. Or he may even completely change the seed and use seed from another farmer in the community instead; though it may still be considered the same maize. Furthermore, the farmer may consider two ears with (to me) seemingly clear morphological differences as the same maize. While this ambiguous and fuzzy varietal concept works fine for the farmers in this study, it does not correspond with the clear-cut definition used in the formal scientific context.

Scientist explains how mental concepts are not simply definitions but dynamic representations that are constituted by the kind of experiences that lead us to acquire the particular concept. This 'sameness' to the farmer is, therefore, not a question of definitions, but is part of the farmer's experience with maize.

Likewise, the farmer's concept of a maize is part of his or her stock of knowledge relating to maize practice. What appears to the outsider to be a fuzzy or ambiguous concept may not appear so to the farmer, who encounters no problems in applying this knowledge in his or her management practices.

For the scientist, ambiguous or dynamic concepts present an important methodological challenge. For example, one may consider the question "How long have you cultivated this maize" a clear and straight-forward question.

The farmer may answer; "Ever since I started farming on my own". Regardless of how many years this refers to, and whether he has mixed it, or completed the seed with other maize during this time, the farmer may consider the maize in question to be the same. In any case, he is not likely to mention any such issues, as this is not how the question was put.

However, from the maize scientist's point of view, it is not the same maize, if its genetic make-up has changed in any noticeable way. Hence, it is important to be aware of differences in concepts or understandings in order to avoid misinterpretations.

These issues highlight the problems in assuming that one can isolate and transfer particular concepts or pieces of knowledge from one 'knowledge context' to another. In other words, a local knowledge concept will not necessarily transfer directly to a scientific knowledge context without problems.

Outside the context from which it is taken, the concept or practice is likely to be reinterpreted against another set of background assumptions. The result is misunderstandings or nonsensical conclusions. This works both ways: the farmers' variety concept does not correspond with the way this concept is used among scientists. Likewise the scientists' concept does not correspond with that of local farmers.

This has implications for research, for example, inrelation to the use of formal questionnaires and specialist categories.Farmers' choice of variety is one of the most important decisions in the cultivation of a crop, since inadequate choice of variety may cause the crop to fail.

On the other hand, if the variety performs well, then its specific traits will broadly influence the quality and quantity of the harvest.

Various factors influence farmers' choice of maize varieties. Even though many farmers in the study communities live and farm under apparently similar conditions, individual preferences, production conditions, and production objectives may vary considerably from one farming household to another.

Bellon lists a series of factors and concerns that may influence farmers' demand for crop and varietal diversity. These include agroecological heterogeneity; concerns regarding risks and uncertainty; resource constraints; concerns regarding labour bottlenecks; management of pests and diseases; maize for the elaboration of special products and foods, and the fulfilment of ritual or social obligations and ties. All of these are also relevant, albeit to varying degrees, in the case of the smallholder maize farmers in the study communities.

CHAPTER – 7

Sources of Seed

It is estimated that 80 per cent of the area planted to maize in Mexico is done so with recycled seed (i.e. seed selected from the previous harvest by farmers, . Selecting seed from one's previous maize harvest and carefully saving it for the next planting season is also a widespread practice among farmers in the study communities, as documented both in the CIMMYT-INIFAP 1998 baseline study and the seed flow tracerstudy carried out in 2002. Of all the farmers who participated in the seed flow tracer study, 75.8 per cent relied entirely on their own seed. Furthermore, as, all respondents claimed to practice seed selection from their own maize harvest.

Selecting and saving seed from one's own maize harvest is clearly a common practice at the household level. Similarly, with regards to the individual seed lot level, researchers still reported that approximately 90 per cent of all seed lots in the study communities were selected by farmers from the previous harvest, while the remaining seed was acquired almost entirely from other farmers, the two communities with the highest percentage of indigenous population, Santa Ana

Zegache and Santo Tomas Mazaltepec, are also the communities that show the least frequency of buying seed (2% and 3% respectively), while San Pablo Huitzo, which has the lowest percentage of indigenous population of all the six study communities, is where the frequency of buying seed is the highest of all (20%). Seed acquisitions are therefore likely to have been in order to complement the farmers' own seed at the time of planting, for experimentation purposes, or, simply to add another kind of maize to one's repertoire.

According to the data from the CIMMYT-INIFAP 1998 baseline study, the main reasons for saving seed from one's own harvest appears to be to secure the seed supply for the following planting and to save money on not having to buy seed from other sources.

Though the combination of seed security and savings also makes up the most important reasons for saving seed in San Pablo Huitzo, respondents in this community appear to be less preoccupied with the combined concerns of seed security and savings. San Pablo Huitzo is also the community where most people save. It is likely that these aspects can be linked to the fact that of the six communities, San Pablo Huitzo is the most prosperous and the community with the largest percentage of irrigation. The latter diminishes the risk of seed loss from a general perspective, and the former means that, even in the case of seed loss, freeing up the resources necessary for seed acquisition is likely to be less of a problem for people in here, as compared to some of the other study communities.

Farmers have various reasons for saving seed from their own maize harvest. One of the things which farmers mentioned first when talking about maize seed practices, whether during focus group discussions or individual interviews, was 'confidence' or 'trust' in one's own maize. This refers to the farmers' notion of trust in the seed they have selected themselves. That is, the belief that the plants germinating from this seed will live up to a certain standardunder the particular production conditions present on the farmers' land.

These circumstances are also reflected in local seed management practices: Farmers chose maize varieties according to a set of characteristics that they perceive as favourable in terms of their own particular needs, knowing the performance of the plants the seed came from under particular agro-ecological and management conditions. For social, cultural and agro-ecological conditions, a variety that may be appropriate for one farmer is not necessarily appropriate for another. Furthermore, by using seed that one knows and trusts, the risk of crop failure due to inappropriate seed is minimized. Hence, what better option to fit one's needs and preferences and to minimize risk, than the seed that one knows and selects oneself.

As many of the farmers commented, once the seed is selected and safely set aside, one can rest assured that the seed for the next planting season is secure. What is more, the seed will be available when it is needed and the farmer will not incur planting delays.

When the time comes, one can therefore avoid spending money and/or time acquiring seed at the last moment before planting, which is when prices typically go up and many small-scale farm households struggle to raise the means necessary for land preparations and planting.

Many farmers set aside more seed than they calculate they will need for their own planting. This provides a buffer against seed loss in storage as well as the possibility to provide seed should another farmer approach them with this request. In the case of sharecropping, which is a common arrangement, the standard procedure is that the landowner provides the land and the seed, while the sharecropper does the work.

Furthermore, for some of these farmers, the family's maize seed is associated with a certain affection value. The seed may be an inheritance, passed on from parents to children when the latter start farming independently.

Usually, the seed is given to a young couple by the man's parents.

In some cases, however, they may receive seed from both parents, and occasionally only from the woman's. Some farmers furthermore regard it as their duty as parents to provide maize seed for their children when they decide to begin farming independently. As one male farmer said: "There has to be seed for the children! That is one's obligation as parents."

This aspect surfaced many times during individual interviews, but it was also mentioned by farmers during focus group discussions. On these occasions both male and female farmers talked about receiving maize seed from their parents together with instructions about how to maintain it and care for it. Some of the participants saw this as a betrothal [*un gran compromiso*], because this maize acts as a memory of their parents, who asked them always to maintain it. For example, one woman described an occasion when as a young child she went with her mother to the market in Ocotlán where they bought white maize for planting. Afterwards her mother said to her: "Remember this maize, that we bought together, do not let it disappear." She promised her 25 In the cases we know of, where this occurred, it was either because he did not have any relatives in the community, because they did not have seed to give, or because of bad relations between the couple and the man's family. The case of Lucio and Felicitas is an example of the latter. Lucio's parents did not want to acknowledge the marriage between the two.

They did not offer seed to the young couple, who on the other hand, did not want to ask for it. Instead they received seed for their first maize crop from Felicitas' parents. mother, and now, many years later, her mother long since passed away, she still preserves the white maize they bought together in Ocotlán.

In some cases farmers even said that they only continue to plant a particular kind of maize in order not to lose it. This is, for example, the case of Valentino and Florentina, a couple in their sixties, who grow mostly *pinto* maize and some yellow, in addition to beans and *maguey*. Valentino says he doesn't really like the yellow maize because it is very late [*tardón*], that is, he considers its growing cycle to be relatively long. However, he explains, they still plant itso as not to lose the seed, because his parents gave it to him and he promised them never to stop planting it.

Thus, for many of the small-scale farmers in the Central Valleys, maize seed is something they have in trust, which links them with previous generations, and which they, in turn, must pass on to their descendants. Often, the seed has been in the family for many years during which it has provided the sustenance of family members, whereby it acquires an inherent affection or symbolic value beyond its immediate utility in the farming system. Saving seed, therefore, becomes a way of conserving and honouring important personal ties. If the parents have passed away, other relatives or foster parents will normally provide maize seed for the first planting.

Finally, saving seed is strongly associated with being 'a good farmer'. In their own way, each of the above mentioned aspects represents part of what constitutes the local concept of 'a good farmer', a notion which, to a certain extent, is comparable to the concept of '*bonus pater familias*' 26 of Roman law.

A good farmer is expected to take good care of his/her seed, and people who do not save maize seed are sometimes frowned upon. As the female farmers in one of the focus groups stated when explaining that a good maize farmer should not lose the seed: is like hurting one's pride for being a good farmer – it is like a humiliation!" On the other hand, though, it is acceptable and legitimate to obtain seed from other farmers in a bad year, or for want of trying out other kinds of maize germplasm, provided the farmer receivingthe seed is generally thought to "take good care" of his/her seed.

In this case, the person is someone who has a justifiable need for the seed and not someone, who prefers to rely on others for seed, rather than make the effort of selecting and storing seed from the previous harvest. In other words, this person 'deserves' the seed and will appreciate the favour.

Interestingly, while the practice of selecting and saving seed from one year to another can be compared to a social norm in the case of maize, of which 26 *Bonus Pater Familias* ('good father of family') is a legal concept referring to a certain standard of reason and conscientiousness applied when estimating a person's guilt. A bonus pater familias is expected to act with reason and care. The concept can be applied to practically all categories of persons, professions, and ages in terms of whether or not the person in question behaved in a reasonable and conscientious way under the given circumstances disregard is associated with a certain stigma, this does not appear to happen in the case of other crops, such as beans or chickpeas. In other words, whereas losing one's maize seed can be embarrassing, especially if it happens several times, losing one's bean seed does not seem to matter. Similarly, some farmers attach a special value of affection to their maize seed, which does not seem to apply to other crops.

Sometimes farmers will talk about people who do not save seed as lazy. However, in most cases, not saving seed is not a voluntary or deliberate decision. For example, in situations where this is linked to crop failure, the farmer did not decide not to save seed. Nevertheless, under certain circumstances not saving seed can be a deliberate or conscious decision by the farmer, and may even form part of his/her normal management practices. For example, whenplanting maize for feed production such as silage or specifically for the production of *elotes* or corn-on-the-cob, the farmer will often harvest everything while the plants are still green, not leaving anything for seed production.

Furthermore, in the cases where hybrid maize is used, the farmer may be aware of the benefits of buying fresh seed for every planting. However, except for these aspects, it is few farmers in the study area who deliberately decide not to bother with seed selection and instead prefer to buy seed from others every year. , this is only the case for between 1 and 2 per cent ofthe farmer maize's in the study communities, except for San Pablo Huitzo. The persons who come back year after year to buy seed from him, do not want to invest time in seed selection and they do not appear to care much about what kind of maize they are planting.

Once in a while farmers also decide to abandon a particular kind of maize; that is, they decide to deliberately stop growing it. This can be motivated by different reasons or considerations, including change of agro-ecological conditions, such as the sale of a plot of land with particular agro-ecological conditions; changes/degeneration over a period of time in the characteristics of the maize in question, for example, the development of a thicker cob, change in colours etc.; or maybe the farmer decides to substitute it for another kind of maize which he/she considers superior. The case of Ana María and Rodolfo and the white maize from Ocotlán, mentioned above, is an example of the latter. Market considerations may also play a role in farmers' abandonment of varieties.

Seed Acquisition

The alternative to saving one's own seed is to acquire seed from a third party. Seed acquisition is an opportunity to obtain maize with desired traits, but, as discussed elsewhere, it also entails risks; either of outright crop failure due to poor or inappropriate seed, or the risk of the maize having less desirable traits.

When trying out another kind of maize, the farmer may cultivate the new maize for one or more seasons before a decision is made on whether to adopt it.

If the new maize is to the farmer's liking it may either be adopted as new maize for cultivation and added to the farmers repertoire of individual maizes being cultivated; or, alternatively, it may substitute an existing maize, or the seed of new maize may be mixed with seed of one of the existing maizes. Thelatter was mentioned above as partial seed replacement, and is often used by the farmers in an effort to obtain one maize with a combination of desired traits from several maizes. Below the issue of experimentation is discussed in more detail.

The second most common reason for acquiring seed is when a farmer commences to farm, which accounts for 27 per cent of the seed acquisitions. This is obviously the case when a new farmer starts farming on an independent basis.

However, it may also be the case when farmers, who for some reason, for example, temporary migration, decide not to plant maize for some time. Due to the relatively fast decline in maize seed germination rate and vigour, the person who wants to take up maize farming again may have to start over again, acquiring maize seed from other farmers, family or yet other sources. However, in many cases it is only some of the household members who migrate (e.g. the husband and/ or grown up children), in which case the wife and other relatives often look after the farm and continue planting the land, for example, with the assistance of hired help or a sharecropper. Lorenzo Benito's case is an example of the latter: After several years as a farmer in Zegache, with a break in which he worked briefly in the US, and another during which he served as the interim President of the Municipality, Lorenzo Benito Ventura wentto Mexico where he found work as a gardener.

He worked in Mexico for more than 25 years, returning to the village in 1998. Ever since he formed his own household around 1950, Lorenzo has planted a white and a yellow maize, both of which were passed on to him from his father. During the years he lived and worked in Mexico City, he continued to grow the same two maize landraces with the help of a sharecropper from the same village. Therefore, he says, he did not lose the seed until some 15 years ago when the harvest failed completely and he lost both the yellow and the white maize. However, as his brothers cultivated the same maize, passed on from their father, Lorenzo acquired new seed of both the yellow and the white type from them, and because it traced back to the same origin, namely their father's white and yellow maize, Lorenzo considers that he recuperated the same two varieties, that he had just lost.

Since he returned from Mexico City and took up farming again, Lorenzo has added to his maize repertoire a black landrace, which he also obtained from relatives in the community. Seed loss may occur because of low yield or total harvest loss, due to drought, water logging, insect attacks, weeds, hail, lodging, or poor management. In addition, seed may be lost during storage due to insects or rodents. A farmer may not save seed, or at least not enough, because he or she has had to sell or eat everything that was harvested including the seed set aside, as a result of insufficient production, an emergency or a crisis, such as a health problem, an accident. Farmers who produce maize for animal feed may harvest before seed is produced. Obviously, seed loss may also occur as the result of several converging factors.

The relatively low percentage of acquisitions related to seed loss is interesting and less than originally expected. However, when combining with some of the more qualitative data, a possible explanation may be provided. According to informants, seed loss is sometimes associated with laziness, lack of knowledge and inappropriate working practices.

Thus, losing one's maize seed readily translates into a social stigma, even though the cause for seed *Local maize seed knowledge and practices* loss may be beyond the farmer's control. This stigma appears to be linked to the notion of 'good farmer', which I mentioned above. Likewise, never to have lost one's seed is a cause for pride for many farmers. Obviously, this does not motivate people to talk about the occasions on which they may have lost their seed, and it is possible that this influenced the answers to the seed flow tracerstudy. For example, on some of the occasions, informants said they acquired seed because they really liked the seed they were offered; however, it is quite possible that this was not the only reason, and that some of them may not have acquired the seed, had they not also had a real need for it.

Seed loss can be partial or complete. Partial seed loss is when only part of the seed needed for the next planting is lost, and therefore only a portion of what is needed has to be acquired outside the household. Complete seed loss is when all the seed of a particular type of maize is lost. If the farmer wants to replace this maize type, new seed must be obtained. The case of Felipa and Santos presents examples of both partial and complete seed loss, and thus, partial as well as complete seed replacement.

Felipa and Santos live in Albarradas together with two of theirgrown-up sons. They grow two hectares of maize and squash, andone of beans. They also own ten donkeys which they use for carrying firewood and other transportation purposes, and occasionallythey rent the animals out to other farmers, for example, to carry the harvest home from the field, or as transport in the harvest of *magueys*.

Felipa and Santos plant only white maize now. They used alsoto grow a yellow maize, but lost it one year when there was a particularly bad drought. Although she says the yellow maize takes longer to *nixtamalizar*, Felipa likes it very much for the quality of tortilla it makes and she therefore acquired another yellow in 1999. However, this one was lost too, after only two cycles. They did noteven manage to take seed, she explains, because the drought hit when the plants were still very young and they dried out beforeeven setting flowers.

Since then they have continued only with their white maize. Santosreceived this maize from his parents, and he and Felipa have grown it ever since they married. Normally, it is Felipa who sorts the maize ears, separating out the largest and healthiest for seed, and Santos who 'makes' the seed [*hace la semilla*], that is, selects and shells the kernels to be used as seed from the ears that Felipa selected. After this, they mix the seed with dried chilli seed to protect the maize seed from storage pests.

In the same year as they lost the second yellow, they found themselves short of seed for the white, and to complete the quantity of seed needed to finish planting they bought two kilos of white seed maize from Sra. Juana. During the course of the conversation Felipa reveals that actually this was not the only occasion on which she has bought seed from Juana; two years before that, a similar situation had arisen, and they had acquired one *almud* of white maize seed from the same lady. Felipa adds that she is friendly with Juana, and should it happen again in the future, she is confident that Juanawould provide the seed they would request.

Experimentation

The widespread use of experimentation is by no means limited to the farmers in the study communities, but has been documented as a common practice in many places. Though the term 'experiment' is being used, it is important to consider that smallholder experiments are organized quite differently from those of formal research. This is linked to the different worldviews in which scientific as opposed to local knowledge is generally rooted. Scientific knowledge is largely construed within a voluntaristic worldview based on an assumption that it is possible to understand the processes of nature and express its underlying causalities in theory, in order to subsequently manipulate the environment.

Meanwhile, local knowledge is generally rooted in what the authors call an adaptive worldview, in which it is assumed that certain parts of nature and the environment are controlled by forces that are beyond human influence. Rather than manipulate the environment, the approach is to accommodate to it. Scientists compare smallholder experimentation with that of agricultural scientists across a number of criteria. While scientists' experiments are always square or rectangularly shaped, using the same size for each treatment and various repetitions, farmer experiments can be of any shape and of different sizes from one treatment to another with no repetitions. Similarly, while in scientists' experiments careful design and planning is considered essential, and the use of numbers for quantification of findings is important, previous planning of experiments is only sometimes the case in farmer experiments, and analysis is primarily visual with limited use of numbers.

Most importantly, however, is the comparison of the purpose or the beneficiary(ies) of the experiment/research. Bentley and Baker note that scientists' research is done for others, that is, not for the scientists themselves, whereas farmers' experimentation is done for the farmer's own use. In the 'scientific knowledge system' the primary aim of experimentation is the advancement of knowledge. Validation comes from active communication of experimental results to fellow scientists and researchers. By contrast, farmers' experimentation and knowledge is distinctly use- and user-oriented. In addition, farmers' knowledge generation is validated by the final technology users, whereas scientists' research is validated by other researchers. Biggelaar notes that farmers in Rwanda did not consider experimentation as separate from everyday agricultural activities, as is the case in the 'scientific knowledge system'.

Box draws attention to the importance of curiosity and play in technological change. With reference to farmers' experiments in the Dominican Republic, as well as in the Netherlands, he points to curiosity and playfulness as far more important in the generation of knowledge than is often assumed. Scientist claims that this aspect of knowledge generation has not been given due attention by researchers. "The reason we know so little about it, is that many experiments are not discussed, either because they are secret, or because they are considered 'play'. Arguing that agricultural knowledge often is generated in the interaction between curiosity and utility, Box calls for what he refers to as a 'non-utilitarian approach to knowledge', that is, an approach which is not focusing only on utilitarian factors such as yields, income or food security, but which includes the notion of fun and playfulness. This is not to say that the utilitarian aspects of experimentation are not important, and farmers' primary concern is still their livelihood. However, the point is that a lot of the experimentation that leads to knowledge generation and technological change, whether by farmers or by researchers, originates in people's curiosity and fascination with 'gently playing with nature – for the fun of it'.

While farmers often experiment because they find it interesting and 'fun', for small-scale farmers in many parts of the developing world, it is also an important element in the efforts of adapting to an ever changing context. For example, reporting from an in-depth study on knowledge generation processes in agroforestry systems in Rwanda, Biggelaar notes that farmers' experimentations were an integrated part of their strategies to overcome ecological and economic uncertainties and a way of exploring opportunities for a better and more secure livelihood. The author even comments that "there was an implicit understanding that not experimenting with new ideas would lead to stagnation and would compromise an already precarious existence".

Sources of Seed

Clearly the reasons to save maize seed are multiple and complex. They cannot be seen just as a simple narrow decision to save money, but must be understood as a practice that has different cultural, economic and agroecological components. As has been pointed out in this and the previous sections, seed is a flexible and negotiable concept. According to local standards it is important to take good care of one's maize seed and for some it is a matter of personal pride.

Maize seed, in particular, seems to be loaded with special symbolic values for many farmers in the study area. A fundamental difference between using one's own seed and acquiring seed from other sources is knowledge. By using seed, which one selected from one's own previous harvest, one has first hand information about the characteristics of the maize in question as well as its management and performance under the particular circumstances where it was cultivated. Furthermore the farmer knows exactly when and how the seed was selected, and how it was stored, and finally one can assume that even the consumption related characteristics of that particular maize are well known by the farmer's household. In contrast, seed from external sources is often associated with different degrees of limited knowledge, though it can provide a solution to urgent seed needs.

In addition, seed from other sources can provide new and interesting traits. Due to the lack of transparency, external seed will always be accompanied by a lack of information. The supplier may know the quality of the seed and provide reliable information on, for example, the ability to germinate. If the supplier is local then he or she may also be able to provide information on the environmental adaptation and production characteristics. But many production traits of a maize can only be expressed verbally in very general terms, and as such the accompanying information is limited unless the farmer has seen the maize cultivated, which is sometimes the case with seed from local sources.

Experimentation is a knowledge building process. During this process new observations, experiences or findings are added to, challenge and/or further contribute to one's current knowledge base. Farmers' experimentation is not something that is limited to a few innovative farmers. Just as Biggelaar (1996) found that experimentation was part of normal farming practices for Rwandan farmers, it is a wide-spread practice among farmers in the study area.

In fact unless a maize comes from a very well known source, such as close family, and the farmer is already very familiar with the maize, then the most common form of introducing a new maize is to plant it in a small area first, that is, to make an experiment.

Informal experimentation provides farmers with firsthand information about the characteristics and the performance of particular maize types under specific agro-ecological and management circumstances. This information is largely based on performative and not verbalized knowledge. As such it is more comprehensive and more easily absorbed and adapted to the farmers other farming knowledge and practices. Upon evaluating the experiment, the farmer has a relatively good basis for deciding whether the maize type in question is appropriate in relation to his or her production objectives. This coincides with the point made above, that farmers' informal experimentation is use- and user-oriented.

From the various examples of farmers' seed acquisitions and experiments, it is clear that regardless of their economic or educational standing, many of the farmers who participated in this study enjoy experimenting and 'trying out' different kinds of maize, even in circumstances where chances of good performance are unlikely. At the same time, farmers' experimentation contributes to local knowledge generating processes. Furthermore, though farmers' small-scale experiments may imply a certain risk, at the end of the day they serve to reduce the risk of major failure. In other words; while they are often motivated by curiosity and playfulness, farmer experiments also serve the purpose of both knowledge generation and risk control: that is, their purposes are both utilitarian and 'for fun'.

CHAPTER – 8

Farm Seed Management Practices

From a population genetics point of view, in the seed selection process farmers exercise selection pressure in an attempt to enhance favoured traits in their maize and lessen the influence of undesired ones. This ensures that certain traits are passed on to the next generation at a higher frequency. Furthermore, these traits are what define a variety in the eyes of farmers, and studies have argued that this selection process plays an important part in what structures diversity in farmers' fields. As demonstrated by the scientists the dynamics of maize genetic diversity in the study area is a combination of geneflow and selection; without farmers' seed selection, maize populations in this region would not show the great morphological diversity observed.

Farmers' maize seed selection can take place at any time between harvest and the next planting. The period of time in which seed selection takes place can vary greatly; in some households it is an intense, focused activity of relatively short duration. However, in many households it is an activity that takes place little by little over a long period of time, that is, for several months.

Finally, some farmers organize their seed selection in a more step-wise fashion, whichcan take place over different periods of time, according to the convenience and traditions of the individual farm household. Both men and women participate in the different steps of the seed selection process, although, in some cases, depending on the household, it is regarded as the responsibility of someone in particular.

In the baseline study an attempt was made at quantifying the use of different seed selection practices and the results of this. Farmers' use of plant characteristics in relation to seed selection has been reported from other traditional agricultural systems, for example sorghum and pearl millet in Africa.

It is noticeable that only some three per cent do any preharvest selection, which means that most are only selecting on the traits of the ear and kernels, but not, for example, on the characteristics of the plant (or the length of the cropping season). This appears to be the common practice for farmer maize seed selection in Mexico.

These traits may, however, have been included when the seed was acquired in the first place. The baseline study investigated the use of four post-harvest selection practices:

1. The separation of the harvest in piles designated for seed or grain.
2. The selection of ears for seed and the subsequent shelling.
3. Selection of seed in connection with using the maize for consumption.
4. Selection of seed just before planting.

The post-harvest selection can be undertaken in different ways. However, a general feature that all have in common, is that selection is done as a twostage process, first selecting the ear, and then selecting the seed kernels within the ear.

One way is to separate the harvested ears into two groups: one for seed and another for grain. The farmers may store the seed as ears with the husk intact until shortly before planting; or, alternatively proceed to dehusk and shell it and store the seed as kernels. Rather than carry out the seed selection as a separate process it may also be done little bylittle, as the harvest is being used. In this case, as the family members use of the stored maize, they will separate out the best ears for seed selection. Finally, the actual selection of the individual kernels to be used as seed may be done just before the planting.

Valdeflores, the predominant combination is to separate the harvested ears into two groups and then shell them before storage. This is complemented by selection as the maize is being used. In Santa Ana Zegache the predominant selection method indicated is during use, and in San Pablo Huitzo the main method is the separation of ears into two groups. Finally, in Santo Tomás Mazaltepec and San Lorenzo Albarradas farmers often select seed when usingthe harvest. However, this is combined with other methods, and no single method or combination of methods is predominant. It should be noted that the processes of post-harvest seed selection and management often take place during a time span of several weeks or even months, and despite several efforts at categorizing or systematizing, in many cases it is not a neatly ordered process that can easily be divided into separate phases.

Selecting the Ears

In local seed management, seed selection depends on the individual farmer's perception of what are desirable traits, and what makes good seed. These criteria are socially constructed, based on local knowledge and passed on between people. It is information, which over time, has been challenged, discussed and maybe modified according to the experience of the individual farmers. Like any other form of technological knowledge, it is a product ofsocial processes in the community. Some households store their maize as ears, leaving the husk on for protection.

Others remove the husk and yet others both de-husk and shell the maize. Initially, all the harvested ears are usually piled up in a certain part of the household or patio, often separated by maize type, if the household in question grows several kinds of maize. A common practice is to undertake a first sorting that separates damaged or badly developed ears from the healthy and well-developed ones. If squash was planted together with the maize and harvested at the same time, it is now put in a separate pile.

The next step is de-husking. On every single ear, the husk is forced open, pulled free and removed from the ear. This is done by hand, leaving the maize ear bare. The quality of the ear is now readily assessed, and in general the farmers who dehusk the maize before storage also use this moment to separate out any badly developed or damaged ears, which in most cases are then set aside to be used for animal feed. Often the farmer also uses this moment to separate particularly 'good' seed ears, for example, for subsequent shelling and storage. In many cases farmers have a clear idea of what the 'ideal' ear of their particular maize looks like, and when selecting seed ears they often try to get as close to this 'ideotype' as possible.

As mentioned above, seed selection is carried out almost exclusively at postharvest and as a result the selection criteria are related almost entirely to the ear and kernel characteristics. The baseline study investigated the different selection criteria applied by the farmers in the region.The vast majority of farmers select for large cleanears with all grains filled. They also look for large clean kernels and grain uniformity.

In San Pablo Huitzo, San Lorenzo Albarradas and Santa Ana Zegache they are also concerned with ear weight, but less so in San Agustín Amatengo, Santo Tomás Mazaltepec and Valdeflores. Cob size is also a concern for just over half of the farmers. Husk cover, which is important both to prevent infestation by pests as well as being an ingredient for example for cooking tamales is of much less concern to farmers. A possible explanation is that themaize types cultivated in the study area generally all have good husk cover, and as such is not an issue in seed selection.

The selection of seed from the individual maize ears also has many similarities across households, although, at the same time the details or sequences may vary quite considerably from one farmer to another. Who is in charge of seed selection also varies from one household to another.

Similar to the selection of ears from which to take seed, many farmers favour large, clean and healthy looking kernels that live up to the individual farmer's idea of what characterizes his/her particular maize, for example, shape, size and colour of kernels. Another common criterion is that kernels that are selected for seed should have intact and spotless pedicels, as damaged or dark pedicels is interpreted as a sign of poor seed quality or doubtful germination ability. As Doña Miriam, explained: As long as it hasits little heart, the white part in the middle, it has to germinate. Look, like this little maize grain, this little heart, and this is where the little maize plant will start . Likewise another woman commented that one must make sure that the seed has been specially selected, is clean and undamaged by insects. Like Miriam, she points out that the 'heart' of the maize seed must be intact.

That one will germinate Many farmers follow a practice of only selecting kernels from a particular part of the ear, for example, only the lower 1/2 2/3 of the ear or only the middle part of the ear. When asked about this practice, farmers normally explain that these kernels make the best seed. Farmers in the study area are ofteninfluenced by a logic of 'like produces like'. For example, according to Don Emilio (Zegache), the maize plants take after the seed it germinates from: if you select only big and beautiful kernels for seed, this is how the maize will be. However, says Emilio, if you use seed that is *guioxito* (small), the maize that will grow from it will be equally *guioxito*.

The kernels at the top of the ear (and often also those at the bottom) are slightly asymmetrical and smallerthan the rest, and in general, farmers in the study area appear to believe that these kernels make a poorer seed and produce inferior plants. A similar thing takes place in relation to the selection of ears for seed selection; farmers choose beautiful, well-developed ears in order for next season's harvest to be one of beautiful, well-developed maize ears. On the other hand, farmers also sometimes experience difficulty in explaining the rationale behind their practice of choice. In that case many simply explain that this is what they were taught about selecting good maize seed, and this is how they have always done it.

Furthermore, the practice of taking seed only from certain parts of the ears appears to be a common practice, not only in Mexico, but also in other parts of the Americas, as well as elsewhere outside the centres of origin of maize. The basis of these practices are not entirely understood.

However, according to Louette and Smale (1998: 11) "the kernels from the ear tip are usually smaller, have poor reserves, and are often damaged by birds, insects, and fungi, which may justify their exclusion". The authors also mention that unpublished results from their own germination tests indicate that the kernels from the upper part of the maize ear demonstrate a slower and a lower germination rate than the kernels of the centre and the base of the ear. With regard to the kernels at the base of the ear, no clear justification for leaving these out from the seed selection exists from a scientific perspective.

However, according to Louette and Smale (1998: 11), as the first silks to appear emerge from the base of the ear, these kernels may be subject to a greater probability of self-pollination and therefore inbreeding, than other kernels.

Seed selection is another area in which maize stands out in comparison to other crops, such as beans or chickpeas. It is common practice among farmers in the study communities to save seed of various crops. However, whereas maize seed is specially selected and generally carefully stored separate from the rest of the maize, thereby constituting an altogether different category from maize grain, a similar practice does not seem to apply for beans or chickpeas.

Miriam explains: "Seed maize is bigger. The little maize kernels, the second class maize, are for eating, but in beans they are the same, there is only one class. This corresponds with Catarina's comment: Beans (seed) are mixed, they are not selected, you throw (sow) it even if it is small or as Liliana said: Even though it is mixed. Yes. It is not selected. In comparison, Eduardo explained that neither beans(seed) nor chickpea(seed), are selected '*revuelto*' (mixed) he stated, adding that If you want to plant chickpeas, you just get it from anywhere.

Harvest and Seed Storage

Storage temperature and seed moisture content are very important for maintaining maize seed quality in terms of germination rate and vigour. In many developing countries, farmers' own seed storage facilities may not be able to control temperatures and moisture levels effectively. As a result seed quality may deteriorate significantly after only one year or less.

Under average local storage conditions in the study area, maize seed can be stored for one to two years and still retain an acceptable germination rate andvigour, provided the maize seed is not damaged otherwise by storage pests, pathogens or fungi. Nevertheless, knowing that seed quality declines with prolonged storage, farmers clearly prefer to use seed that is as 'fresh' as possible.

Most farmers do not store maize seed longer than one or a maximum two seasons and poor germination rate is seldom a problem in relation to the seed the farmer selected him-/herself. However, seed quality remains a point of concern, especially in connection with seed acquisitions from other, unknown sources.

The harvest can be stored either as ears with or without husks, or shelled as kernels. San Pablo Huitzo, Santo Tomás Mazaltepec, San Lorenzo Albarradas, and Valdeflores, the preferred form of storage is as ears, whereas in San Agustín Amatengo and Santa Ana Zegache farmers predominantly store the harvest as kernels. For the latter it is somewhat surprising that on the question of seedselection they also indicated that this was done when using the grain. This must mean that the respondents understand 'use' as including the shelling of the ears before storage.

Farmers in the study area apply a variety of pesticides to protect the maize seed during storage, containing various kinds and concentrations of toxic substances. These include phostoxin, folidol and occasionally, lindane. Of these, the most widely used are the phostoxin tablets, and when used correctly this is also the least harmful to human health. The tablets react with air, dissolving slowly as a gas. The tablets are left among the maize to be stored; however, for the product to be effective, an airtight container must be used in order to contain the gas. Not all farmers who use this product are aware of the way it works. Many store their grain or seed in ordinary sacks or large finely woven baskets; however, as these are not airtight, the effect of the tablets is significantly reduced unless lined with plastic. At the same time, it is quite common that farmers exceed the recommended dosage per volume of maize – sometimes deliberately in order to counter what appears to be a weak effect of the tablets. Nevertheless, some farmers are concerned about the poisonous effect and do not treat the maize intended for consumption. As a female farmer from Zegache exclaimed: "No! If even the gorgojos will not eat it like that – then neither will I!".

When folidol or lindane is applied, it is usually in a powder version. If the farmer stores the seed as whole ears it is common to simply sprinkle the ears with the powder. If the seed is shelled the powder is added and mixed well with the maize.

These methods of protecting seed against storage pests are sometimes also used in grain storage. For example Bernardo explains how he applies folidol when storing the maize harvest: "I store it in the *troje* with the husk and all, and we shell it little by little as we use it. When I fill up the *troje*, I first sprinkle folidol over the bed (wooden bottom of the granary). Then I arrange a layer of ears, sprinkle a bit of water over it and then another sprinkling of folidol. Then I continue with another layer of ears and so on until the *troje* is full or there are no more ears left."

Among artisanal methods, the most commonly mentioned is the application of lime, or in some cases, ashes, which is simply mixed with the shelled maize seed, and provides a certain level of protection against insects. Some farm households also use chilli or herbs to protect the seed against storage pests, for example, Felipa and Santos, mentioned in the section on seed acquisition.

Farmers use a variety of containers for seed storage, although plain nylon sacks are the most common. Some farmers recognize the disadvantages of just using plain sacks and devise their own solutions to grain/ seed storage. For example, Pablo Lopez (Huitzo) stores his maize seed in a tightly sealed barrel/ oil drum, and Doña Rosa (Zegache) uses nylon sacks, but lines them with heavy-duty plastic sacks in order to contain the effect of the tablets she applies against storage insects. Others use heavy-duty plastic buckets withtightly fitting lids, and for very small seed quantities I have also seen emptied soft-drink bottles with screw-lids used.

A smaller number of households in the study communities own a small-scale metal silo specifically designed for small-scale farmers' grain storage. During initial phase of the CIMMYT-INIFAP project farmers complained about the high rates of grain and seed losses in storage. As a response the CIMMYTINIFAP project staff provided training on a series of practices and technologies which could help improve storage conditions and diminish storage losses, including a simple type of metal silo that some farmers in San Agustín Amatengo were already using. The silos were tested in the other study communities and a rotating financial scheme was set up in order to help interested farmers acquire a silo of the preferred dimensions. The principle of the silos is to effectively prevent mice and rats from having access to the maize stored in it, while at the same time protecting the grain against insect infestation. The latter is achieved by making sure that the grain is not infested at the moment when the silo is filled, and subsequently by the lack of oxygen in the full silo.

Where farmers store the maize seed is yet another detail. The granary or *troje* is normally outside the house, but somewhere in the patio where household animals cannot easily get to it. Shelled grain is often stored on the porch, in an outhouse or in connection to the cooking shed/kitchen. However, the prepared (i.e. shelled and possibly treated) maize seed is often stored inside the house or, alternatively, somewhere else considered equally secure.

Some farmers will check the state of their maize seed once or twice during the storage period, cleaning it and removing any infested kernels and maybe re-applying treatment against storage pests.

The widespread practice of selecting seed based on ear and kernel criteria alone, means that traits, which maintenance depends on selection related to other parts of the plant, are left out of the selection process. Obviously, this would also exclude selecting for traits which cannot be seen with the human eye or otherwise easily observed, for example, the contents of lysine and tryptophan in the case of QPM-Maize. Other traits - length of production cycle,or other aspects of the plant - are taken into account at the time when the farmer decides what maize to plant. It is important to keep in mind that this decision, that is to say, varietal selection, has a considerably larger impact on production and consumption characteristics, than does seed selection from one cycle to the next.

On-farm seed management practices are based on performative knowledge, and the above description illustrates a range of issues in trying to verbalize this knowledge. Especially, when looking at the data from the surveys, these problems become obvious. For example, the ambiguity of the term 'in use' made it difficult to understand seed practices in Santa Ana. Almost all answered that they selected the ears for seed when using the maize ; however, they also store the maize as kernels meaning that they shell it before storage . The use therefore refers to the shelling rather than to the use for consumption. This also illustrates the problem of taking a complex activity, such as seed management where the farmers draw on a wide range of knowledge, and apply different options in a flexible manner according to the circumstances, and trying to break this down into a series of yes/no questions.

The seed selection process has been broken down into a numberof practices, and organized in a presumed systematic and chronological way, but this does not seem to appear particularly relevant to farmers and is not in accordance with their perception of seed practices. However, interviewees often tried to accommodate and answer within the options provided.

It should be emphasized here, that the Later in the research process, it became clear that many farmers in the study communities did not organize their seed management practices in a systematic sequence of clearly defined and separate steps. Rather, seed management is done in a parallel and multi-tasked fashion and forms an integral part of harvest management. Many of the initial steps are not seed management ac- 29 Compared to other types of maize, Quality Protein Maize (QPM) contains nearly twice as much of two key amino acids - lysine and tryptophan – which make protein usable for humans and monograstric animals. Quality Protein Maize is considered able to improve the diets of people who consume mainly maize. Furthermore, used as feed, it is assumed that QPM can provide poor farmers with a means for improving livestock production, and thereby, for new income-earning strategies. QPM is grown on more than 0.5 million hectares in 22 developing countries.

It is currently not grown in the study area.Ativities as such, but simply harvest management, where seed selection may occur in an opportunistic manner, whenever one has a moment or comes across particularly good seed material. Seed selection as such is not carried out as one continuous activity where each step is completed in a relatively short, coherent time span. Several parts of the process may be initiated simultaneously and interrupted various times over a total period of several weeks or months. The interruptions are often not motivated by technical issues or seed management considerations, but are much more of a resource management issue, where work is undertaken when time between other tasks and events permits it.

The situation is similar with regards to seed storage practices. The tables presented here could be said to convey a 'deceptionally clear' picture of local seed storage practices. However, as with other harvest and seed management practices, the preparation and organization of seed storage is often undertaken in parallel with, or according to how, other activities or events unfold, much along the lines of Richards' reflections on agriculture as a performance. The issues raised in this section illustrate the problems that were repeatedly mentioned in relation to efforts to 'translate' performative into verbalized knowledge and *vice versa*. The results of such efforts often include categories that appear unclear or ambiguous, and the loss of internal logic as complex processes are broken down into separate elements. In short, as pointed out earlier, efforts to 'translate' one kind of knowledge into another necessarily imply a transformation and often also simplification of the knowledge involved.

The aspects presented here also highlight some of the problems in trying to systematize local knowledge. In a review of the development of the study of local knowledge, researcher explains that early efforts to recognize and incorporate local knowledge into the development debate tended to assume that it could be conceived of as a 'system', a fact which often led to the simplification of local knowledge. As Pottier notes, it has since become increasingly clear that knowledge changes and evolves continuously, not necessarily in a systematic way, nor is it necessarily organized as such.

As a result the notion of 'knowledge systems' and their presumed boundedness is increasingly challenged.

Attempts to organize farmers' seed practices in terms of a seed system encounter difficulties both with regard to the need for defining the constituting elements of the system, such as seed, varieties, and management practices, as well as in relation to defining the boundaries of the system itself. In the findings above I have discussed how both seed, and especially varieties, are flexible concepts that cannot easily be 'fitted into' a clear definition related to an element of a system. Likewise, in presenting the seed management practices, it was clear that many different ways of doing similar tasks exist, and these may be combined in different ways.

The specific choice of practice is often influenced by factors such as availability of labour or the personal preferences of the farmer at a given moment. The seed management practices are also difficult to pin down. Seed selection, for example, has considerable flexibility in terms of when it is carried out, and this flexibility is used by the farmers to complete it as *ad hoc* parts of other practices over an extended period of time. This means that several activities, which in fact are integral parts of other practices, such as post-harvest management, contribute to the same end, for example seed selection. As such, these practices cannot easily be separated from other practices and this leads to difficulties in delimiting the seed system.

In short, several aspects of on-farm seed management practices, including seed selection, form part of general post-harvest management, or are carried out in relation to using the harvest for consumption. Thus isolating or separating seed selection is problematic. Furthermore, seed exchange practices are also embedded in more general social relations, and must be analysed in relation to this more general social network. As such, both on-farm and off-farm seed practices are difficult to isolate as individual, clearly delimited parts of a seed system.

It is possible to construct a system for just about anything and thus it is also possible to consider the Oaxacan farmers' seed practices as a system. However, doing this inevitably implies a gross simplification of local knowledge and a process of 'disambiguation' of farmers' seed concepts. It also leads to difficulties in delimiting the seed system in relation to other practices both onand off-farm.

The widely used term 'informal seed systems' or 'farmers' seedsystems' implies that these should be analysed as systems, but this research questions the very notion. Instead, it is proposed to focus on seed practices, and to ensure that the analysis takes the ambiguities in farmers' seed concepts, as well as the flexibility in their seed practices, into proper account.

Furthermore, it considers farmers' seed practices as integral parts of other onand off-farm practices. Performative knowledge is not only a question of technical and practical skill in relation to undertaking a given activity. As pointed out, the knowledge required often also includes moral dimensions such as,for example, how to promote one's own status, obligations and responsibilities towards others.

The notion of 'status' refers to one's position in society, particularly the position that other people attribute to one, that is, the prestige or importance that one acquires in the eyes of other people. Meanwhile the term 'reputation' refers to the opinion that other people have of someone as a result of what he/she does and how he/she behaves. The two are obviously closely related, yet, high status is not automatically linked to good reputation and *vice versa*.

Social roles are also closely related to status. However, one's status may change depending on the social context – in fact sociologists talk about 'sets of statuses' referring to the individual's various statuses in different social contexts. Often a distinction is made between ascribed status based on biological factors, for example, age, sex, race; and achieved status, which refers to the individual's efforts and achievements in his/her life course. While aspects such as structural positions and roles can be considered human accomplishments, they have real consequences for the people who occupy them.

Social interaction is always situated in time and space and may involve different forms of verbal and non-verbal communication. Everyday interaction depends on subtle relationships between what we convey with our faces and bodies and what we express in words. The ability to interpret and accord meaning to social situations, in order to draw on the role or positional knowledge acquired during socialization, is therefore an important interactional skill, given that improvisation and negotiation are essential features in the construction of social action. The study of how people make sense of what others do and say has been called ethnomethodology.

The metaphor of the theatre has also been used as a framework for the analysis of social interaction and everyday life. This notion also refers to the socially defined expectations of an individual in a given status or social position. Following the theatre metaphor, in the various contexts of social life there tend to be clear distinctions between 'on-stage' and 'off-stage' situations, where actors prepare themselvesfor the performance and relax afterward. A good example of this is Goffman's classic study of self representation in everyday life, where he demonstrates how social actors, playing out their roles, are sensitive about how they are seen by others, and hence try to manage the impressions they give. Impression management can take many forms, the most common probably being the unconscious following of norms, for example, dressing appropriately for a business meeting or for church.

Elsewhere in this chapter the notion of 'the good farmer' which refers, admittedly in a rather nebulous or fuzzy way, to an ideal embodying a series of aspects that are highly valued in others by the farmers in this region, and which includes issues such as personal integrity, independence and respect.

At the same time the idea of 'the good farmer' includes a series of common, local values regarding farming and being a fellow community member touched upon again in subsequent chapters in relation to trust, mutual help and reciprocity).

As a member of the community one is expected to take part in various community issues and *tequios* and contribute one's due share in relation to both actual financial contributions as well as in terms of public service or the responsibilities that one may be appointed to. After several years abroad as a migrant worker, Don Jesus returned to his community, when he was appointed for a public responsibility. Jesus explained that while he saw it both as an honour and an obligation, he also realized that refusing the chargewould eventually have made it very difficult for him to return to the community at a later stage and still be respected as a full community member.

Other community member obligations are easier to negotiate. For example, failure to participate in *tequios* and other community works is often sanctioned, for example by a 'fine' or, eventually, by loss of certain rights, which can then only be regained through compensation. People who know beforehand that they cannot participate, sometimes make arrangements to send someone else in their place, or, as is sometimes done in the case of migrants, monetary compensation is agreed upon with the authorities and sent from abroad or paid by family members in the community. As with other farming practices, certain aspects of seed management seem to influence one's standing and reputation as a 'good farmer'. For example, knowing how to select and manage maize seed appears to be regarded as a valuable and central skill.

People who do not produce their own seed are frowned upon; sometimes even regarded as lazy or not very good farmers. A discussion regarding this issue developed spontaneously during the men's focus group discussion in San Lorenzo Albarradas, during which the majority of the group quickly established that this applied to 'farmers, who don't know how to do their job properly, or who are lazy, do not select and save seedfrom the previous harvest'. Or note Liliana's comment, with a clearly reproachful tone to it: "Why do you ask for seed, if you have maize?!" Likewise, in relation to mutual helpfulness, people, who are known to have plenty of seed, but who are nevertheless not willing to provide seed to others, are thought of as selfish.

Living up to the role of the good farmer also implies not taking undue advantage of another farmer in need: one should be honest and not take advantage of a fellow farmer/villager. This is especially so if the person is in a difficult situation, such as lacking seed in the middle of the planting season. Rodolfo, for example, still held a grudge against the person who sold him seed, but used the occasion to press the price up, on one occasion where he still had land left to plant, but had already run out of seed.

This is consistent with data from the in-depth interviews, revealing what appears to be a strong cultural value in the study area associated with being helpful to others, as long as one is able to do so while covering one's own needs. Likewise, in connection to this, an important motivating factor for many seed providers is that the person requesting the seed has a genuine need for it. This was an aspect, which arose during almost all the focus group interviews. Finally, it should be mentioned that this also appears to be part of a common sense of reciprocity.

For example, there are aspects of 'the good farmer' which have more to do with social and cultural values than strictly with farming, for example, being helpful towards others, doing one's fair share of community work, taking part in reciprocity and exchange, and answering to social obligations in general.

With specific regard to farmers' maize seed practices, this is expressed in the custom of saving seed, as well as in relation to a common sense of social responsibility which includes being willing to supply seed to a fellow farmer in need, as far as one is able to, and one is generally pressed to do this and other favours in a way that does not take undue advantage of the other farmer's need.

Like much other performative knowledge related to seed practices, the issues of how to be a good farmer and community member, and gain others' respect clearly influence people's practices. This is often reflected in the strategic representation of local knowledge and in people's individual self-representation.

The way farmers present their local knowledge is influenced by the situation in which they find themselves and by whom they are communicating with and who else is present, but also by how the farmers would like to present themselves. Hence, farmers often do not only represent what they do, but also what they would like to be doing. For example, when describing particular practices or different aspects of community life, many had a tendency only todescribe the 'good' version, that is one which is, if not ideal then at least acceptable according to local codes of practice and interaction. Meanwhile, the 'bad' or less acceptable version is always about other people.

Methodologically these are not aspects that are prone to surface, for example, in the application of formal questionnaires. Rather, these and similar issues are better illuminated through the use of more qualitative approaches. The degree to which, in this research, farmers 'negotiated' their representation of local knowledge in a strategic way is difficult to estimate.

The long term interaction with CIMMYT researchers, at different intensities and intervals and through a wide variety of modalities, as well as thetransparent approach adopted by the institution with regard to research objectives and resources, no doubt served to establish a certain trust and credibility in the relationship between farmers and researchers. However, there is little doubt that some degree of negotiation did take place, both by farmers and by researchers, seeking to explore the possibilities of furthering one's chances of obtaining favours, information, prestige and so forth. Still, this does not necessarily affect research in a negative way - after all this is the usual way, in which knowledge processes and much communication betweensocial actors take place.

CHAPTER – 9

Seed Dormancy

Seed dormancy is a condition of plant seeds that prevents germinating under optimal environmental conditions. Living, non dormant seeds germinate when soil temperatures and moisture conditions are suited for cellular processes and division; dormant seeds do not.

One important function of most seeds is delayed germination, which allows time for dispersal and prevents germination of all the seeds at same time. The staggering of germination safeguards some seeds and seedlings from suffering damage or death from short periods of bad weather or from transient herbivores; it also allows some seeds to germinate when competition from other plants for light and water might be less intense. Another form of delayed seed germination is seed quiescence, which is different than true seed dormancy and occurs when a seed fails to germinate because the external environmental conditions are too dry or warm or cold for germination. Many species of plants have seeds that delay germination for many months or years, and some seeds can remain in the soil seed bank for more than 50 years before germination. Some seeds have a very long viability period, and the oldest documented germinating seed was nearly 2000 years old based on radiocarbon dating.

True dormancy or innate dormancy is caused by conditions within the seed that prevent germination under normally ideal conditions. Often seed dormancy is divided into two major categories based on what part of the seed produces dormancy: exogenous and endogenous. There are three types of dormancy based on their mode of action: physical, physiological and morphological.

There have been a number of classification schemes developed to group different dormant seeds, but none have gained universal usage. Dormancy occurs because of a wide range of reasons that often overlap, producing conditions in which definitive categorization is not clear. Compounding this problem is that the same seed that is dormant for one reason at a given point may be dormant because of another reason at a later point. Some seeds fluctuate from periods of dormancy to non dormancy, and despite the fact that a dormant seed appears to be static or inert, in reality they are still receiving and responding to environmental cues.

Exogenous Dormancy

Exogenous dormancy is caused by conditions outside the embryo and is often broken down into three subgroups.

Physical Dormancy

Which occurs when seeds are impermeable to water or the exchange of gases. Legumes are typical examples of physically dormant seeds; they have low moisture content and are prevented from imbibing water by the seed coat. Chipping or cracking of the seed coat or any other coverings allows water intake. Impermeability is often caused by an outer cell layer which is composed of macrosclereid cells or the outer layer is composed of a mucilaginous cell layer. The third cause of seed coat impermeability is a hardened endocarp. Seed coats that are impermeable to water and gases form during the last stages of seed development. Mechanical dormancy.

Mechanical Dormancy

Mechanical dormancy occurs when seed coats or other coverings are too hard to allow the embryo to expand during germination. In the past this mechanism of dormancy was ascribed to a number of species that have been found to have endogenous factors for their dormancy instead. These endogenous facts include physiologically dormancy cased by low embryo growth potential.

Chemical Dormancy

Includes growth regulators etc, that are present in the coverings around the embryo. They may be leached out of the tissues by washing or soaking the seed, or deactivated by other means. Other chemicals that prevent germination are washed out of the seeds by rainwater or snow melt.

Endogenous Dormancy

Endogenous dormancy is caused by conditions within the embryo itself, and it is also often broken down into three subgroups: physiological dormancy, morphological dormancy and combined dormancy, each of these groups may also have subgroups.

Physiological Dormancy

Physiological dormancy prevents embryo growth and seed germination until chemical changes occur. These chemicals include inhibitors that often retard embryo growth to the point where it is not strong enough to break through the seed coat or other tissues. Physiological dormancy is indicated when an increase in germination rate occurs after an application of gibberellic acid (GA3) or after Dry after-ripening or dry storage. It is also indicated when dormant seed embryos are excised and produce healthy seedlings: or when up to 3 months of cold (0-10°C) or warm (=15°C) stratification increases germination: or when dry after-ripening shortens the cold stratification period required. In some seeds physiological dormancy is indicated when scarification increases germination.

Physiological dormancy is broken when inhibiting chemicals are broken down or are no longer produced by the seed; often by a period of cool moist conditions, normally below (+4°C) 39°F, or in the case of many species in *Ranunculaceae* and a few others, (-5°C) 24°F. Abscisic acid is usually the growth inhibitor in seeds and its production can be affected by light. Some plants like Peony species have multiple types of physiological dormancy, one affects radicle (root) growth while the other affects plumule (shoot) growth. Seeds with physiological dormancy most often do not germinate even after the seed coat or other structures that interfere with embryo growth are removed. Conditions that affect physiological dormancy of seeds include:

- *Drying:* Some plants including a number of grasses and those from seasonally arid regions need a period of drying before they will germinate, the seeds are released but need to have a lower moister content before germination can begin. If the seeds remain moist after dispersal, germination can be delayed for many months or even years. Many herbaceous plants from temperate climate zones have physiological dormancy that disappears with drying of the seeds. Other species will germinate after dispersal only under very narrow temperature ranges, but as the seeds dry they are able to germinate over a wider temperature range.
- *Photodormancy* or light sensitivity affects germination of some seeds. These photoblastic seeds need a period of darkness or light to germinate. In species with thin seed coats, light may be able to penetrate into the dormant embryo. The presence of light or the absence of light may trigger the germination process, inhibiting germination in some seeds buried too deeply or in others not buried in the soil.

- *Thermodormancy* is seed sensitivity to heat or cold. Some seeds including ocklebur and amaranth germinate only at high temperatures (30°C or 86°F) many plants that have seed that germinate in early to mid summer have thermodormancy and germinate only when the soil temperature is warm. Other seeds need cool soils to germinate, while others like celery are inhibited when soil temperatures are too warm. Often thermodormancy requirements disappear as the seed ages or dries.

Seeds are classified as having deep physiological dormancy under these conditions: applications of GA3 does not increase germination; or when excised embryos produce abnormal seedlings; or when seeds require more than 3 months of cold stratification to germinate.

Morphological Dormancy

Embryo underdeveloped or undifferentiated. Some seeds have fully differentiated embryos that need to grow more before seed germination, or the embryos are not differentiated into different tissues at the time of fruit ripening.

Immature embryos - some plants release their seeds before the tissues of the embryos have fully differentiated, and the seeds ripen after they take in water while on the ground, germination can be delayed from a few weeks to a few months.

Combined Dormancy

Seeds have both morphological and physiological dormancy.

Morpho-physiological or morphophysiological dormancy occurs when seeds with underdeveloped embryos, also have physiological components to dormancy. These seeds therefore require dormancy-breaking treatments as well as a period of time to develop fully grown embryos.

- Intermediate simple
- Deep simple

- Deep simple epicotyl
- Deep simple double
- Intermediate complex
- Deep complex

Combinational Dormancy

Combinational dormancy occurs in some seeds, where dormancy is caused by both exogenous (physical) and endogenous (physiological) conditions. some *Iris* species have both hard impermeable seeds coats and physiological dormancy.

Secondary Dormancy

Secondary dormancy occurs in some non-dormant and post dormant seeds that are exposed to conditions that are not favourable for germination, like high temperatures. It is caused by conditions that occur after the seed has been dispersed. The mechanisms of secondary dormancy are not yet fully understood but might involve the loss of sensitivity in receptors in the plasma membrane.

Not all seeds undergo a period of dormancy, many species of plants release their seeds late in the year when the soil temperature is too low for germination or when the environment is dry. If these seeds are collected and sown in an environment that is warm enough, and/or moist enough, they will germinate. Under natural conditions non dormant seeds released late in the growing season wait until spring when the soil temperature rises or in the case of seeds dispersed during dry periods until it rains and there is enough soil moisture.

Seeds that do not germinate because they have fleshy fruits that retard germination are quiescent, not dormant.

Many garden plants have seeds that will germinate readily as soon as they have water and are warm enough, though their wild ancestors had dormancy. These cultivated plants lack seed dormancy because of generations of selective pressure by plant breeders and gardeners that grew and kept plants that lacked dormancy.

Seeds of some mangroves are viviparous and begin to germinate while still attached to the parent; they produce a large, heavy root, which allows the seed to penetrate into the ground when it falls.

CHAPTER – 10

Informal Seed Exchange

Research in the Central Valleys indicated that farmers who needed to acquire seed from other farmers experienced some difficulty in finding seed that met their requirements. First, a farmer has to learn who grows which maize variety and investigate the characteristics and performance of the maize of interest. Then he or she must make sure that the information offered is trustworthy and the seed is reliable. Finally, the conditions of acquiring the seed must be negotiated.

It therefore appears that acquiring seed of diversemaize varieties under these conditions can entail risks and high transaction costs to individual farmers. If one assumes that there is a high probability of seed loss due to climatic conditions and poor storage, then it is reasonable to hypothesize that a group of farmers could maintain more diversity than any individual, at a lower cost and with reduced probability of loss.

There should be clear incentives for individual farmers to cooperate in providing seed and information for a diverse set of maize varieties—in other words, for engaging in collective action to support their seed supply. The basic ingredients for collective action are present: a group of farmers with a common interest and a benefit that accrues from a voluntary group action. Furthermore, in this region several traditional collective action institutions exist, such as the *tequio* To test this hypothesis, the following operational definition of collective actionwas developed, based on the notions of collective action reviewed earlier:

> The actions of a well-defined group of farmers linked by a set of rights and responsibilities regarding the mutual supply of seed of a diverse set of farmer varieties.

Building on this definition, the following predictions were developed in order to examine the hypothesis.

This is reasonable because rainfed agriculture predominates in the area, with common occurrence of severe drought. For example, during the period of the study 1997-2002 there were two years with major droughts (1997 and 2001). Furthermore, drought and storage losses were identified as very important concerns by these farmers. *Téquio* refers to a form of comunal work in which one has to provide a service to the community.

It can refer to comunal work in the interest of a certain group (for example, the local school), or it can be in the interest of the community in general (for example, construction and maintenance of roads, drinking water, infrastructure, or sewerage). *Guelaguetza* is a Zapotec institution of mutual aid between households. It can take place in many different situations and between different people and includes agricultural tasks, the roofing of houses, weddings, funerals, and religious festivals.

The existence of a number of people that identify themselves as part of a group that recurrently shares seed in some form (e.g., sale, exchange, or barter).

- Apart from the existence of a group, collective action could be inferred from adherence to a certain set of rights and responsibilities regarding the mutual supply of seed. This behaviour should be reflected in how seed transactions are conducted (e.g., specific practices or patterns associated with seed flows).

- The existence of collective action should depend on providing certain advantages or benefits to farmers compared to working individually. These could include lower transaction costs for acquiring seed or reduced risk of seed shortages. Saving seed from one's own harvest is the predominant practice in the study area. Previous research showed that 89.7 per cent of all seed lots were saved by farmers from their own previous harvest, and the rest were acquired from other farmers. Only 24.2 per cent and 20.9 per cent of the farmers in the tracer study acquired or distributed seed, respectively, in 2001. Farmers in the tracer study said that their main reasons for acquiring seed were for experimentation and, to a much lesser extent, to overcome the lack of seed of their own. The main reason for giving seed to others was a sense of social responsibility.

Farmers felt that they were morally obliged to give seed to the farmer who asked for it. Most transactions involved the exchange of money or seed, and some farmers said explicitly that they engaged in seed transactions to obtain seed or money, but often the reason to engage in the transaction was not the payment *per se*. Many types of seed transactions were identified.

Types of Seed Transactions

Informants described different types of seed transactions in detail during the ethnographic interviews and focus group discussions. Quantitative data on seed transactions were later gathered in the seed flow tracer study. Transactions were classified into seven categories, including 'other', which referred to infrequent, *ad hoc* transactions.

The quantitative data clearly show the heterogeneity of transactions, although purchases account for half of all transactions. Focus group discussions and informant interviews provided detail on the many types of transactions and their individual variations. The hypothesis predicted a relatively uniform and clearly defined mode of transaction, reflecting adherence to a set of rights and responsibilities and a system of collective action. This was not what was found. In addition, although most informants remembered from whom they had obtained seed in the recent past, many had difficulty recalling to whom they had given seed, which may explain the noticeable discrepancy between the number of acquisitions and distributions.

Most seed transactions carry no obligation beyond the immediate transaction, except for borrowed seed or seed given as a gift. The borrower must repay the seed, and gifts usually carry an implicit obligation to return the favour. Transactions involved different types of social relations between the seed.

Purchase is the form of transaction least dependent on the social relation between the two parties. In fact farmers in general say that this type of transaction can be done with any person. This is confirmed by the findings from previous CIMMYT studies in the region. The exception would be the farmers who will only distribute seed to other farmers if they are confident that this other person will observe the general norm of taking good care of the seed and be very careful not to lose it again. Of all the farmers interviewed for this study in particular, none had any reservations with regards to selling seed to others, provided they could spare the seed and were appropriately compensated. In Frida's household for example, they cannot spare much maize, whether grain or seed, and in general they do not sell. Only if another family member or a very close friend asks, but then just 2 3 kilos, no more says Frida.

According to Pablo H. the person who needs to acquire seed will approach a possible seed provider. Then he asks: 'Will you sell me a bit of maize seed?' One then says yes or no. If there is seed, then 'yes, only, you will have to pay so and so'. And if there is not, then one says 'I haven't got any [seed], but I have maize grain, but it is good, it is big, almost the same as the seed.' Then it's up to the other person.

It should be pointed out that in this region the price of local maize seed is about twice the price of grain, while the price of a commercial hybrid will be in the order of 8-10 times the price of grain.

Lending Seed

Some types of seed transactions are normally only done with people the seed provider knows and trusts. The least common is lending, meaning that the seed provider hands over the seed and is promised by the receiver, that he/she will give back the same quantity and quality of seed, once the harvest is ready; or as Camilo put it: You give it to me now, and when I harvest I will replace it for you! . This type of transaction is not very common and is usually restricted to very close friends, compadres or kinship relations. Catarina, for example, was very clear on this: Only with my mom.

Hybrid seed costs several times the price of local seed and can normally not be acquired in the communities. However, the price of the seed, - whether land race, hybrid or other, is still minimal compared to other production costs. That is, though probably the most important input, the seed is also one of the cheapest. Nevertheless, farmers often state the price of hybrid seed as a reason for not using it. Furthermore, farmers normally emphasize that hybrid varieties need more water than local maize landraces and longer time to mature. Finally, but maybe most importantly, for their own consumption these farmers prefer local landraces. When hybrids are sown, it is mostly for animal fodder or, in smaller quantities, for *elotes*, i.e. corn-on-the-cob, a popular snack.

From the word *compadrazgo,* referring to a ritual kinship somewhat similar to the relation known elsewhere as godparents, through which close relations of loyalty, mutual help, reciprocity, and confidence are established and formalized. Often there is a certain degree of prestige associated with being asked to become someone's *compadre* or *comadre,* and in some ways *compadrazgo* can signify social capital. Informants stress the issue of trust as very important in this case.

That's where people's friendships come in – not just anybody is going to lend you something like that. It will be because they trust you are going to give it back says Pablo L. The reason is obvious: this type of transaction implies a risk for the seed provider that the receiver of the seed will forget, or not be able to fulfil his/her part of the deal, which is, to give back same quantity and quality of seed after the first harvest.

Exchanging Seed

Another type of transaction is exchange of seed. Josefina explains this transaction in the following way: If you bring one almud of white maize [seed], we will exchange it for one almud of black maize [seed] *'a cambio'* (in exchange). If one wants black, if one wants yellow, *belatove* . . . the colour one wants, you go and bring your maize (seed).

Exchange appears to be less problematic than lending. The 'handover' and 'payment' takes place at the same time, and the seed provider avoids the risk of not being paid. Nevertheless, judging from these and other interviews many seed providers still have some reservations about exchange. The issue seems to be the uncertainty about whether the provider receives seed of a satisfactory quality in return for his/her seed. While selling/purchase does not seem to present a problem for most seed providers, obtaining the money to pay for the seed can be a problem for somefarmers seeking seed.

They may have an advantage in exchange or lending instead of purchasing. However, unless the person asking for the seed is trusted, seed providers tend to prefer selling/ purchase as the type of transaction, as this helps them avoid the risks of lack of payment or of receiving low quality kernels in return for their own specially selected seed.

The in-depth interviews and focus group discussions revealed the categories of social relations frequently involved in seed transactions. These were later quantified in the tracer study. The seed provider categories mentioned here do not constitute an exhaustive list, and each category could be divided into subcategories with overlaps and variations among them. For example, neighbours can sometimes also be relatives or *compadres*. This grouping reflects the informants' own classifications; that is, if an informant referred to a seed provider as an uncle, the provider was classified as a family member, though the person might also be a neighbour.

Family members and acquaintances are the most common sources or recipients of seed. Most seed transactions took place between people who already knew each other and shared a feeling of mutual obligation. Informants in focus group discussions and ethnographic interviews were not able to identify specific persons as particular seed-relations (except for researchers involved in the CIMMYT/INIFAP project, which included a seed distribution activity).

The data regarding social relations do not provide evidence of farmers' involvement in specialized institutions or groups for the mutual supply of seed.

Relationship Between Social Relations and Seed Transactions

Trust is important for these farmers. Trust in the seed may often derive from a relationship of trust between the recipient and the provider.

The data suggest a systematic relationship between transaction type and supplier-recipient relationship . Inheritance and gifts are the most common transactions among kin. While purchase is common among all social relationships, it isclearly the most common among strangers and acquaintances. It seems that as social distance between supplier and recipient increases, the frequency of purchases increases and the frequency of gifts and inheritance decreases.

In barter and exchange among acquaintances and strangers, informants also said that quantities were calculated based on market prices, but rates in transactionswith kin or a close relationship might be more favourable. Clearly no particular type of transaction is restricted to a single category of seed supplier. Closeness of social relationship improves chances of preferential treatment a finding that is consistent with Sahlin's (1972) findings on primitive exchange but it does not determine the type of transaction.In interviews as well as focus group discussions, informants emphasized that seed must be of good quality and appropriate for target production conditions and preferences. Some seed seekers also take into consideration the way the seed has been cultivated and what they know about the general quality of a supplier's work.

These complex requirements make it difficult for those seeking seed to obtain appropriate information. The problem is exacerbated by the lack of a generally accepted and clearly defined nomenclature for local maize varieties, beyond broad categories such as grain colour, grain size, and growing cycle, as described in previous research in the area and confirmed by both Zapotec- and Spanish-speaking farmers in thepresent study.

The easiest source of knowledge and trustworthy information, not surprisingly, is the people with whom the farmer already has close social relations. Farmers may already know the characteristics of varieties used by kin or close friends, and they can easily obtain more information. Conversations with family members, compadres, and neighbours, as well as observations of what other farmers were growing, were among the most frequently reported ways of obtaining information about seed used elsewhere in the community.

Acquiring seed from trusted sources reduces the risk of obtaining inappropriate seed. Similarly, seed transactions can occur through many types of social relationships, so farmers are not dependent on a single supplier. *Frequencies of seed transactions* It is difficult to assess the frequency of seed transactions. Farmers do not keep records of such transactions, and estimates must rely on the memories of those interviewed.

In the tracer study, seed transactions involving current cultivars were carefully registered, noting the year they took place and allowing farmers to go as far back in time as desired. Recent transactions are more likely to be remembered than those from a long time ago. Notwithstanding these limitations, an estimate of the frequency of seed transactions was calculated.

The distribution between acquisitions and instances of providing seed is approximately the same, meaning that on average acquisitions occur 0.31 times every year and provisions 0.39 times a year (in both cases, approximately once every three years). In 2001 only 24.2 per cent and 20.9 per cent of farmers in the tracer study engaged in seed acquisitions and distributions, respectively. Seed transactions are apparently infrequent and do not involve a large number of farmers every year.

Three parameters were identified to analyze the presence of collective action among farmers to access seed of a diverse set of maize landraces:

1. a group of farmers;
2. rules or practices; and
3. derived benefits.

Within these three parameters, the expected collective action was not found. First, if a farmer is a member of a group related to seed supply, one would have expected informantsto be able to name particular people whom they rely upon to obtainseed time after time. This was not so. In many cases, farmers had trouble remembering the people with whom they had had transactions. While many seed transactions take place within prior existing social relations, most seed transactions do not involve any direct long-term obligations between suppliers and recipients, as would have been expected in a specialized organization or group. In other words, while individual farmers participate in groups, networks, or other organizations, none of these networks appear to revolve specifically around issues related to seed supply. In fact, it is when farmers experience problems related to seed that they draw on existing networks and social relations to identify possible solutions.

Second, there were many types of seed transactions. The diversity of transactions, even under similar circumstances, as well as their bilateral nature, suggests that there is no fixed procedure or otherwise clearly defined frame *Collective action in informal seed exchange* work for seed transactions, whereas a collective action scenario would involve a set of relatively well-defined practices. Seed needs, and hence transactions, do not seem to have a special status. They appear to be just another resource that farmers occasionally share with each other as part of the arrangements that make life possible in rural areas.

The transactions are not governed by specific seed-related rules but are negotiated in the wider context of the social relation between the involved parties, so the particular details of the transaction may depend on many issues that may not be related specifically to seed.

For example, the seed provider may give favourable treatment to those he considers very close relations, regardless of whether the issue is seed, a request for labour, or the loan of farm implements.

Third, no clear benefit seems to be associated with collective action. Part of the rationale for the original hypothesis was that seed loss was the principal driving force behind seed transactions and that collective action would reduce the problem of seed loss. The results showed that this is not the case—seed loss does not seem to be a major problem for these farmers—and a more important driver for acquiring seed is farmers' experimentation. Clearly experimentation is a form of managing risk to acquire information, but it is related to curiosity and the search for new maize types that fit farmers' needs.

When farmers occasionally do obtain seed from other farmers, it is mainly from close social relations. There are good reasons for this. The cost of obtaining information on different varieties and availability of seed should be relatively low, given that it can be obtained as part of normal, frequent social interactions.

The social ties give rise to trust and confidence that the seed has the desired characteristics and quality. At the same time, farmers often have first-hand knowledge of the varieties grown by relatives or friends. If the variety is grown in the same community under conditions similar to those in the farmer's own fields, uncertainty related to environmental adaptation is reduced.Finally, obtaining seed from a close social relation can often securepreferential treatment in the transaction. Close social relations are an important but not exclusive source of seed for farmers, however. Farmers do get seed from people outside their family circle, particularly through purchase.

This variation in seed sources emphasizes the flexible and sometimes *ad hoc* nature of seed transactions among farmers. Given the low frequency of seed loss, the current seed dynamics, in whicheach farmer maintains and reproduces one or more landraces and only infrequently engages in a seed exchange, appear relatively resilient in terms of maintaining local crop genetic resource diversity.

Nevertheless, these dynamics depend on sufficient opportunities for obtaining seed from others when the need arises. At the moment this does not appear to be a major limitation, but future changes to the production system may alter this. For example, a sharp drop in the number of maize farmers, due to migration or shifting to other crops, could limit the efficacy of the current practices for maize seed acquisition, particularly if individual farmers assume that others are maintaining certain seed types but nobody actually does so.

Farmers generally save seed from one crop cycle to the next. The need to acquire new seed is therefore occasional rather than constant or recurrent. The incentives for collective action may be low because the fixed costs may exceed the benefits, given the relatively low frequency of acquiring seed off of the farm.

Rather than maintaining collective action for seed supply, farmers mobilize social resources on an *ad hoc* basis to solve a problem of seed shortage or to take advantage of an interesting opportunity for accessing new seed.

Farmers' seed management in the study communities entails very low transactions costs, and the seed available through existing social relations is sufficiently reliable to prevent seed loss from being a major problem. Collective action would have to bring very considerable benefits to improve on this.

Within the three parameters identified for examining collective action, this was not found to be an important element in farmers' local seed practices. However, the mobilization of social relations plays a crucial part in relation to farmers' seed transactions, and the types of seed transactions are not random, but should rather be seen as the outcome of a negotiation which in turn may reflect certain rules within a social group.

The way collective action was operationalized here could be considered quite restrictive: it is confined to formal organizations with very strict group membership with the sole purpose of supporting seed flows.

Its advantage, however, is that it provides very specific predictions to test. Even if these are rejected, it provides a rigorous opportunity to learn and reassess the hypothesis and associated assumptions.

One could alternatively consider the existence of more informal institutions with rules that are not predetermined and that adjust to contingencies. These 'fuzzy' rules are more difficult to identify, but they are also more flexible and better suited to deal with risk and uncertainty (for example, crop failure or storage problems). Add to this the desire to experiment. Under these circumstances, it would be reasonable to conclude that elements of collective action in other spheres play an indirect role in seed exchange. One has to be careful, however, not to interpret any outcome of a negotiation in a social group as evidence of collective action, since this could dilute the concept to a degree where almost any activity that is not undertaken in a social vacuum would become a form of collective action.

From a methodological perspective, the findings presented here provide suggestions for other studies regarding collective action. It is important to identify certain minimum criteria to use as indicators for the presence of collective action in a particular context. Furthermore, the specific issue or problem in relation to which collective action is being considered, and the affected population, should be clarified at an early point in the research.

In the initial discussion of the concept of collective action, two approaches were identified: one which is based on the view of collectivities as social entities and another which starts from the perspective of the individual social actor.

This study suggests that the point of departure of further studies of informal seed exchange should be the ways and processes through which individual farmers deal with issues and concerns related to seed and the incentives they face to act individually or collectively.

One can hypothesize that collective action in seed supply may be quite important in circumstances where seed loss is frequent and widespread and where farmers acting as a group may increasetheir individual chance of accessing seed when needed (e.g., areas that suffer frequent, but patchy droughts so that not everybody is affected at the same time), or where there is an interest or need for seed of diverse crop types but information about this diversity may be very difficult to gather, as in environmentally heterogeneous areas with very low population density.

Several other issues also merit further study. For example, if collective action does not play a primary role in the organization of maize seed dynamics in these communities, then what does? How does informal seed supply actually work? What are the organizing principles that underlie local seed supply and help shape farmers' practices? Likewise, it would be interesting to understand the extent to which issues regarding the availability of and access to seed of a diverse set of maize varieties are perceived as a limiting factor and whether or not they influence farmers' transaction costs in relation to seed acquisition.

An important implication of the findings presented here is the challenge that certain issues would present to the development of a commercial seed sector in this area of Mexico.

The demand for seed from external sources, whether seed of improved or farmer varieties, is small. Furthermore, these farmers have different needs and preferences and therefore require different maize types. One size does not fit all (or at least 'a few sizes do not fit all'). Interventions such as those practiced in the CIMMYT/INIFAP research project demonstrated farmers' interest in acquiring seed of other maize varieties.

As part of that project, farmers purchased seed of many diverse maize varieties, but only in small quantities and for experimentation. As mentioned earlier, 2,726 kg of seed were sold to 371 farmers, but the average amount purchased was around 4.3 kg. To sell one ton of seed, almost 250 transactions are required.

This may not be such a problem if the demand is only for one or two varieties, but if the demand is for many different varieties, the costs of selling seed may be too high for a commercial provider. Supplying seed under such circumstances may not be a self-sustaining enterprise, since commercial seed enterprisesmost likely have to supply larger quantities of fewer varieties to be financially viable.

Finally, interventions based on collective action to support farmers' efforts to maintain maize diversity in this region, such as establishing community seed banks, may not be successful. Interventions directed more towards individual farmers, such as the CIMMYT/INIFAP research project, or which build on local institutions that serve other purposes, may be more effective.

CHAPTER – 11

Agricultural Biodiversity

Agricultural biodiversity is a sub-set of general biodiversity. It includes all forms of life directly relevant to agriculture: rare seed varieties and animal breeds (farm biodiversity), but also many other organisms such as soil fauna, weeds, pests, predators, and all of the native plants and animals (wild biodiversity) existing on and flowing through the farm. However, most attention in this field is given to crop varieties and to crop wild relatives. Cultivated varieties can be broadly classified into "modern varieties" and "farmer's or traditional varieties". Modern varieties are the outcome of formal breeding and are often characterized as 'high yielding'. For example the short straw wheat and rice varieties of the Green Revolution. In contrast, farmer's varieties (also known as landraces) are the product of (breeding and) selection carried out by farmers. Together, these varieties represent high levels of genetic diversity and are therefore the focus of most crop genetic resources conservation efforts. Agricultural biodiversity is the basis of our agricultural food chain, developed and safeguarded by farmers, livestock breeders, forest workers, fishermen and indigenous peoples throughout the world. The use of agricultural biodiversity (as opposed to non diverse production methods) can contribute to food security and livelihood security.

Although the term *agricultural biodiversity* is relatively new - it has come into wide use in recent years as evidenced by bibliographic references - the concept itself is quite old. It is the result of the careful selection and inventive developments of farmers, herders and fishers over millennia. Agricultural biodiversity is a vital sub-set of biodiversity. It is a use of life, i.e. ancillary biotechnologies, by Mankind whose food and livelihood security depend on the sustained management of those diverse biological resources that are important for food and agriculture. As for everything, agricultural biodiversity can be used, not used, misused and even abused. Agricultural biodiversity includes:

- Domesticated rop and 'wild' plants (called: crop wild relatives), including woodland and aquatic plants (used for food and other natural resources based products), domestic and wild animals (used for food, fibre, milk, hides, furs, power, organic fertilizer), fish and other aquatic animals, within field, forest, rangeland and aquatic ecosystems.
- Non-harvested species within production agroecosystems that support food provision, including soil micro-biota, pollinators and so on.
- Non-harvested species in the wider environment that support food production agroecosystems (agricultural, pastoral, forest and aquatic ecosystems).

However, agricultural biodiversity, sometimes called Agrobiodiversity.

"Encompasses the variety and variability of animals, plants and micro-organisms which are necessary to sustain key functions of the agroecosystem, its structure and processes for, and in support of, food production and food security". It further "comprises genetic, population, species, community, ecosystem, and landscape components and human interactions with all these".

Aquatic diversity is also an important component of agricultural biodiversity. The conservation and sustainable use of local aquatic ecosystems, ponds, rivers, coastal commons by artisanal fisherfolk and smallholder farmers is important to the survival of both humans and the environment. Since aquatic organisms, including fish, provide much of our food supply as well as underpinning the income of coastal peoples, it is critical that fisherfolk and smallholder farmers have genetic reserves and sustainable ecosystems to draw upon as aquaculture and marine fisheries management continue to evolve.

Unusual Strains of Maize are Collected to Increase the Crop Diversity When Selectively Breeding Domestic Corn

Genetic erosion in agricultural and livestock biodiversity is the loss of genetic diversity, including the loss of individual genes, and the loss of particular combinants of genes (or gene complexes) such as those manifested in locally adapted landraces. The term genetic erosion is sometimes used in a narrow sense, such as for the loss of alleles or genes, as well as more broadly, referring to the loss of varieties or even species. The major driving forces behind genetic erosion in crops are: variety replacement, land clearing, overexploitation of species, population pressure, environmental degradation, overgrazing, policy and changing agricultural systems.

The main factor, however, is the replacement of local varieties by high yielding or exotic varieties or species. A large number of varieties can also often be dramatically reduced when commercial varieties (including GMOs) are introduced into traditional farming systems. Many researchers believe that the main problem related to agro-ecosystem management is the general tendency towards genetic and ecological uniformity imposed by the development of modern agriculture. Pressures for that ecological uniformity on farmers and breeders is caused by the food industry demand for more and more raw materials consistency.

Human Dependency

Agricultural biodiversity is not only the result of human activity but human life is dependent on it not just for the immediate provision of food and other natural resources based goods, but for the maintenance of areas of land and waters that will sustain production and maintain agroecosystems and the wider biological and environmental services (biosphere).

Agricultural Biodiversity provides:

- Sustainable production of food and other agricultural products emphasising both strengthening sustainability in production systems at all levels of intensity and improving the conservation, sustainable use and enhancement of the diversity of all genetic resources for food and agriculture, especially plant and animal genetic resources, in all types of production systems.
- Biological or life support to production emphasising conservation, sustainable use and enhancement of the biological resources that support sustainable production

systems, particularly soil biota, pollinators and predators. Ecological and social services provided by agro-ecosystems such as landscape and wildlife protection, soil protection and health (fertility, structure and function), water cycle and water quality, air quality, CO_2 sequestration, etc.

Comparisons of Cropping Systems

The general trend noticed by the analysis of biodiversity present in different cropping systems (e.g., industrial agriculture and organic farming) was that a greater the diversity of crops (temporally and spacially) resulted in a greater overall biodiversity of the agroecosystem, though this is not always the case. A meta-analysis of studies comparing biodiversity noted that, when compared to organic cropping systems, conventional systems had significantly lower species richness and abundance (30% greater richness and 50% greater abundance in organic systems, on average), though 16 per cent of studies did find a greater level of species richness in conventional systems Another study found that cropping systems that required heavy use of chemical amendments (e.g., the widespread broadcasting of pesticides and glyphosate, a practice ubiquitously found throughout the United States and Canada) had significantly greater levels of pollination deficits, whereas organic fields of the same crop (Canola) witnessed no pollination deficits . Other cropping systems like permaculture have undergone little study to determine relative levels of biodiversity compared to other cropping systems, but because they continue to reinforce the goals of increasing overall crop biodiversity, it can be extrapolated that an even greater level of biodiversity would be observed.

Agroecosystems *vs.* Natural Ecosystems

Agricultural biodiversity has spatial, temporal and scale dimensions especially at agroecosystem levels. These agroecosystems - ecosystems that are used for agriculture - are determined by three sets of factors: the genetic resources (biodiversity), the physical environment and the human management practices. There are virtually no ecosystems in the world that are "natural" in the sense of having escaped human influence. Most ecosystems have been to some extent modified or cultivated by human activity for the production of food and income and for livelihood security. However there are no places that cannot be returned to the natural landscape.

Bibliography

Pressoir, G. and Berthaud, J. (2004). Population Structure and Strong Divergent Selection Shape Phenotypic Diversification in Maize landraces. *Heredity,* 92(2): 95-101.

Pretty, J. and Smith, D. (2004). Social Capital in Biodiversity Conservation and Management. *Conservation Biology,* 18 (3): 631-63.

Putnam, R.D. (1993). The Prosperous Community. Social Capital and Public Life. *The American Prospect,* 4 (13).

Putnam, R. D. (1995). Bowling Alone: America's Declining Social Capital. *Journal of. Democracy,* 6 (1): 65-78.

Putnam, R. D. (1996). The Strange Disappearance of Civic America. *The American Prospect,* 7 (24).

Quiroz, C. (1996). Local Knowledge Systems Contribute to Sustainable Development. *Indigenous Knowledge Monitor* 4 (1).

Rack, M. (2003). Interfaces of Knowledge: The Revival of Temples in West Hunan, China. In: Pottier, J.; Bicker, A.; Sillitoe, P. (Eds.), *Negotiating Local Knowledge. Power and Identity in Development.* Pluto Press. London. Sterling, Virginia.

Ravnborg, H. Munk (1993). Targeting International Agricultural Research Towards the Rural Poor. *CDR Working Paper, 93.4.* Centre for Development Research, Copenhagen.

Ravnborg, H. Munk (1996). *Agricultural Research and the Peasants. The Tanzanian Agricultural Knowledge and Information System*. Centre for Development Research, Copenhagen.

Ravnborg, H.M.; Cruz, A.M. de la; Guerrero, M.P.; Westermann, O. (2002). Collective action in Ant Control. In: Meinzen-Dick, R.; Knox, A.; Place, F.; Swallow, B. (Eds.), *Innovation in Natural Resource Management. The Role of Property Rights and Collective Action in Developing Countries*. Johns Hopkins University Press. pp. 257-271.

Remington, T.; Walsh, S.; Charles, E.; Maroko, J.; Omanga, P. (2002). Getting Off the Seeds-and-Tools Treadmill with CRS Seed Vouchers and Fairs. *Disasters*, 26 (4): 316-328.

Rice, E.; Smale, M.; Blanco, J. L. (1998). Farmers' Use of Improved Seed Selection Practices in Mexican Maize: Evidence and Issues from the Sierra deSanta Marta. *World Development*, 26 (9): 1625-1640.

Richards, P. (1985). *Indigenous Agricultural Revolution: Ecology and Food Productionin West Africa*. Hutchinson, London and Westview Press, Boulder.

Richards, P. (1989). Agriculture As A Performance. In: Chambers, R.; Pacey, A.; Thrupp, L.A. (Eds.) *Farmer First: Farmer Innovation and Agricultural Research*. Intermediate Technology Publications Ltd., London, UK.

Ritchie, S.W. and Hanway, J.J. (1982). *How a Corn Plant Develops*. Special Report No. 48. Iowa State University of Science and Technology. Cooperative Extension Service, Ames, Iowa.

Ritzer, G. and Goodman, D. J. (2003). *Sociological Theory*. 6th Edition. McGraw-Hill, New York.

Rohrbach, D.D. (1997). Farmer-to-farmer Seed Movements in Zimbabwe: Issues Arising. In: Rohrbach, D.D.; Bishaw, Z.; Gastel, A.J.G. van (Eds.), *Alternative Strategies for Smallholder Seed Supply*. Proceedings of An International

Conference on Options for Strengthening National and Regional Seed Systems in Africa and West Asia. March 1997, Harare, Zimbabwe. ICRISAT, India.

Rucht, D. (2002). Summary of the Main Results and Identification of Research Questions. Discussant's Comments. Cultural Diversity, Collective Identityand Collective Action - Consequences of the Opening up of National Borders.

Ruiz Garcia, Aida (2002). *Migración Oaxaquena. Una aproximación a la realidad.* Coordinación Estatal de Atención al Migrante Oaxaqueno. Oaxaca,Mexico.

Sahlins, M.D. (1968). Tribal Economics. In: Sahlins, M.D.: *Tribesmen.* Englewood Cliffs, New Jersey.

Sánchez, J.J.G.; Goodman, M.M.; Stuber, C.W. (2000b). Isoenzymatic and Morphological Diversity in the Races of Maize in Mexico. *Economic Botany* 54: 43-59.

Index

P

Q

R

S